HARVEST FROM THE VINEYARD

Lessons Learned from the Vineyard Symposiums

DARROCH "ROCKY" YOUNG AND DR. HELEN BENJAMIN

A Publication of the Community College League of California

A Publication of the Community College League of California

ISBN: 0692721274
ISBN 13: 9780692721278
Library of Congress Control Number: 2016908746
Seaway Publishing
Port Ludlow, WA

About the Authors

DARROCH "ROCKY" YOUNG

D arroch "Rocky" Young retired as chancellor of the Los Angeles Community College District in 2007. In retirement, he is currently working as the chief consultant for the Collaborative Brain Trust (CBT), a subdivision of McCallum Group, Inc., and has recently authored a book on leadership[1]. In addition to numerous speaking engagements related to his book, Rocky also recently completed a strategic planning assignment at Monterey Peninsula College. Previously, he provided consulting services on strategic planning to numerous colleges, including Oakland Community College (MI), College of Western Idaho (ID), West Valley-Mission Community College District (CA), Contra Costa Community College District (CA), Grossmont-Cuyamaca Community College District (CA), Rancho Santiago Community College District (CA), MiraCosta College (CA), and Citrus College (CA). Furthermore, for each of the last eight years, Rocky has been working for the Community College League of California, coordinating and overseeing the annual New CEO Workshop and the Vineyard Symposium (for experienced CEOs) in Napa Valley.

---

[1] *A Walk Through Leadership*, available through Amazon.com

As chancellor, Rocky initiated the first formal comprehensive strategic planning effort in the district's history. Under Rocky's leadership, the district solved its financial problems. Rocky also launched a major Student Success Initiative aimed at improving all student educational outcomes across the district-including student graduation, transfer, and job placement rates. He initiated an aggressive districtwide marketing campaign to publicize community college educational opportunities and revamped the district's enrollment management programs.

Before assuming districtwide responsibilities, Rocky was president of Pierce College, a position he took in 1999. Under his leadership, the college increased its enrollment by 51 percent in less than three years, making it one of the fastest growing community colleges in California. He put a master plan in place that included extensive community involvement, created a new 15-week semester plan that has become the most replicated academic calendar in California, and reversed years of financial difficulties to create healthy financial reserves for the college. In addition, Rocky fostered new partnerships with Caltech, UCLA, UC Berkeley, and CSU Northridge as well as a number of industry partners in the private sector. He also created strong alliances for the college with neighborhood groups, businesses, and elected officials.

Prior to coming to Pierce College, Rocky served as vice president of academic and student affairs and vice president of planning and development at Santa Monica College where he created the concept for the Santa Monica College Academy of Entertainment and Technology, formed partnerships with 50 entertainment firms, and led the effort to receive the Board of Governors' approval of the Academy as an educational center. In addition, he created the Transfer Alliance Program with UCLA, developed a high school dual enrollment program with local unified school districts, and created the college's first Master Plan for Education, Comprehensive Facilities Master Plan, and the Master Plan for Technology.

Rocky was awarded the 2007 Harry Buttimer Award as the outstanding community college executive in California, the 2003 Pacesetter of the Year by the National Council of Marketing and Public Relations, the 2003 Steve Allen Award for Excellence in Education, and the 1998 ACCCA Leadership Award for Administrative Excellence in California Community Colleges.

DR. HELEN BENJAMIN

Since 1972, Dr. Helen Benjamin has served as an educator in secondary and higher education. She currently is the chancellor of the Contra Costa Community College District (District) located in the San Francisco Bay Area and is passionate about student success and endeavors to create an educational environment conducive to learning. She was appointed to the position in 2005 and is the first African American and the first woman to hold the permanent position since the District's establishment in 1948.

Helen first served as the dean of Language Arts and Humanistic Studies at Los Medanos College in 1990 and has held progressively higher level positions, including vice chancellor, educational programs and services; interim president at both Los Medanos College and Contra Costa College; and permanent president for Contra Costa College. Her career began in Dallas, Texas, where she served as a high school English teacher before returning to her alma mater, Bishop College, as an assistant professor of English and department chair, followed by service as division chair of Communications and Humanities at Cedar Valley College in the Dallas County Community College District.

Helen has been acknowledged for her leadership skills and working with a team to bring positive change. In her current position, her successes have been many, including moving the District from a dire financial situation to building and maintaining healthy reserves, responding to operational revenue declines with offsetting operational budget cuts, and dramatically increasing the funding of long-term, historically unfunded liabilities; moving the District from an adversarial bargaining environment to interest-based; providing leadership for the passage of two facility bond measures totaling $736M; and championing the needs of the underserved.

Helen is committed to maintaining an active role in a wide variety of professional and community organizations. At the local level, she serves on the Kennedy-King Memorial College Scholarship Fund, a countywide effort to provide District students of color with financial support to continue their education at the four-year or graduate level. At the state level, she has served as chair for numerous statewide accreditation visiting teams; as president of both the California Community Colleges Chief Executive Officers and the board of the Community College League of California; and as chair of the CEO California Promise Leadership Team. At the national level, she holds the distinction of being the first community college representative appointed by Congress to the Advisory Committee on Student Financial Assistance. She served as convener of the Presidents' Round Table of Community College African American CEOs and on the board of the American Association of Community Colleges. She currently serves on the board of Excelsior College in Albany, New York.

Helen has received many accolades for her service through the years. Recent honors and awards include the following:

- the Harry Buttimer Distinguished Administrator Award;
- 2014 Mentor of the Year by the National Council on Black American Affairs;
- one of 20 community college CEOs from throughout the country to participate in the first White House Summit on community colleges;
- member of the Higher Education delegation to South Africa by invitation of the People to People organization;
- Woman of the Year by the California Legislature, 14th Assembly District, and the City of San Pablo; and
- Woman of Distinction by the East Bay Business Times.

Helen holds a B.S. degree in English from Bishop College in Texas and earned master's (Educational Supervision) and doctoral degrees (English) from Texas Woman's University in Denton, Texas.

Table of Contents

Table of Contents

Introduction

T
he first Vineyard Symposium was organized by David Wolf and Steve Weiner in 2001. David Wolf had a long career in community colleges that included, among many faculty and administrative positions, serving as president of West Los Angeles College and Pierce College. He was also the provost for the California Maritime Academy and, prior to his retirement in 2001, he completed a five-year term as the executive director of the Accrediting Commission for Community and Junior Colleges (ACCJC) within the Western Association of Schools and Colleges (WASC). Over the years, David developed a close friendship with Steve Weiner, whose connection with California community colleges was less direct but no less important. Steve served as a professor in the Graduate School of Education at both Stanford University and U.C. Berkeley as well as the dean of the Graduate School of Education at U.C. Berkeley. His connection to community colleges grew closer during his eight-year term as the executive director of WASC and as the president of the California Community Colleges Board of Governors.

When David retired, there was time for the two of them to think about ventures they wanted to pursue together in retirement to help improve community colleges and higher education in general. These eventual endeavors included the creation of the Campaign for College Opportunity (2002), Common Sense California (2004), and the Endowment for California Leadership (2008). However, their first joint effort upon David's retirement was to create and host the Vineyard Symposium for college presidents and chancellors in 2001.

The idea for the retreat was started by David Wolf and Steve Weiner when they became increasingly aware that college CEOs had little opportunity for engaging in confidential discussion with people who fully understood the complexity of colleges and the pressures under which CEOs operate. Throughout the history of the symposium and including current practice, the format is structured around topics with which the participants are currently wrestling. The symposium strives to create a level of sincere, honest dialogue that is both comforting and renewing. Further, the purpose of the symposium is to provide a retreat setting which will support a few powerful days of in-depth discussions about the nature of the presidency, the challenges of the job, how to renew one's self and stay enthusiastic, how to deal with adversity, how to make significant decisions, and how to move through the "passages" of the presidency toward retirement. Also, in that it is often very difficult for CEOs to form relationships with other CEOs, it is felt that if the symposium created the appropriate environment, it would tend to create professional relationships that would last throughout a CEO's entire career and beyond.

The very first Vineyard Symposium was held at Stanford University and hosted by Jim March, a professor in the Graduate School of Education at Stanford, who joined David Wolf and Steve Weiner as a facilitator. The first symposium invited eight CEOs from two-year colleges all over the United States.

Since the first symposium was so successful, the decision was made to continue the symposium; however, a different site was needed. In order to create the right environment, the symposium needed to be held at the right location. This is where David Wolf reached out to another of his long-time friends, Chris McCarthy, who had just become the president of Napa Valley College. Chris suggested and made the arrangements for the retreat to be held at the Mont LaSalle Christian Brothers Retreat Center in the hills above Napa. David and Steve liked the location, and Chris joined the effort as one of the rare frequent participants. Chris handled all retreat arrangements. The Mont LaSalle Retreat Center has been the site of the symposium ever since.

From 2002 to 2005, David and Steve were joined by Roy Lawson, president of Hope International University, to help facilitate the symposium. They also kept experimenting with different compositions of participants. For these three years, the participants were split evenly between community college presidents and four-year college and university presidents. The number of participants was limited to eight. In 2006, the decision was made to invite only permanent community college presidents and chancellors – a practice which has remained ever since.

At some point, it became necessary to find a more cost-effective means of offering the symposium, yet, keep the number of participants small. As a result, each symposium was restricted to a maximum of 13 participants, with a target of 12 people, which corresponds to the limitations on accommodations at the facility. Furthermore, in an effort to serve as many CEOs as possible, CEO participation is limited to only one symposium per CEO.

It has been the philosophy of the symposium to use experienced CEOs as facilitators. In 2007, David Wolf and Steve Weiner, as well as Roy Lawson, decided it was time for them to hand over the symposium to new people. Subsequently, Diane Woodruff, former president of Napa Valley College and former interim state chancellor, and Kevin Ramirez, former president of Sierra College, joined Chris McCarthy to form the new group of hosts and facilitators for the symposium. In 2009, with the unexpected death of Chris McCarthy[2], Rocky Young, former chancellor of the Los Angeles Community Colleges, was invited to be the third facilitator. In 2012, Diane and Kevin decided it was time for them to make a change, and, subsequently, Helen Benjamin, chancellor of the Contra Costa College District, and Sandra Serrano, chancellor of the Kern County Colleges, joined Rocky to form the group that serves as the current facilitators for the symposium. It should also be noted that in 2007, the Community College League of California joined as a sponsor of the Vineyard Symposium, and they have maintained that sponsorship to the present day.

It has been the experience of the facilitators that a little preliminary "homework" by participants seems to lubricate the symposium's conversation and process. Each year, part of that assignment is to read *Leadership Blues*. *Leadership Blues* was an opinion piece written, in part, by Steve Weiner. It is over ten years old, and might be slightly outdated, but it is included for participants' reading as a means to stimulate thinking about the presidency and as a way to honor the tradition of the symposium.

After reading *Leadership Blues*, each participant is required to write an essay describing "what's waking you up at night?" All CEOs are facing challenging leadership roles, but some issues are more worrisome than others. Each participant is asked to write a summary of his or her most worrisome current leadership challenges. All communications are treated as strictly confidential and for the Vineyard Symposium participants only. The essays help to begin the sharing process and help the facilitators build the agenda for the symposium.

Over the years, after working with over 125 different CEOs, the facilitators have noticed there are certain challenges or issues that seem to appear in one form or another almost every year. Each challenge is unique because of the CEO and the college;

---

[2] The Vineyard Symposium was subsequently named the Chris McCarthy Vineyard Symposium to honor the memory of Chris McCarthy.

nevertheless, there is a common theme to these repeated issues. Of course, every year also has many unique challenges. However, having noticed the repetitive nature of a subset of issues among such a large sample of CEOs, the facilitators felt it would be useful to share them with a broader audience since they undoubtedly represent systemic challenges facing most leaders in the community college system.

The Vineyard Symposium has a strict rule of confidentiality, so the description of the repetitive challenges and issues are written in a way that does not associate them with any one CEO. In any event, these challenges reoccurred so many times that they could not be attributed to only one or two presidents.

The real benefit of this writing effort may be in preparing the list of repetitive challenges. There is no right answer to these challenges, but we have tried to offer suggestions based on how we have dealt with them in our leadership roles. Our responses are meant only as suggestions. When these issues were discussed in the symposium, they involved a more active inquiry process, which is the nature of the symposium. Yet, it seems inappropriate for us to not at least offer whatever help we can to the reader. Since these challenges are most likely universal, it is hoped organizations, districts, and colleges will follow-up this publication with discussions of their own on these challenges and generate even better ideas, solutions, and suggestions. It should also help current leaders who are presently facing one or more of these challenges to recognize they are not alone. We have all had to deal with them at one time or another.

It is important to note in each chapter that we do not offer a complete discussion of the broad topic, but, instead, we focus only on the specific issue repeatedly presented by CEO participants. For example, in Chapter 2, Accreditation, we do not provide a complete discussion of all areas and issues with accreditation.

Instead, we simply discuss the accreditation issues that were repeatedly raised.

Since the symposium is attended by experienced CEOs, the symposium has never been intended to be an educational forum to train CEOs. It only focuses on issues that are causing problems for experienced CEOs, and, therefore, our publication discusses only those issues.

The symposium is attended by college presidents in single- and multi-college districts and by district chancellors. Accordingly, in each response to an issue, it would probably have been more accurate to always refer to college/district in order to cover all situations. However, that made it very cumbersome to read, so college has been predominantly used to represent both CEO assignments.

For those readers who are former participants in the Vineyard Symposium, some of these issues may help you to recall the time you spent in Napa. For those of you who have not participated, it is hoped these writings will encourage you to participate in the future. The Vineyard Symposium is a wonderful, unique experience for CEOs that should be experienced by every CEO in California.

The original intent of this publication was to have it authored by all three of the current facilitators – Rocky Young, Helen Benjamin, and Sandra Serrano. Unfortunately, while Sandra did participate in the early stages of the writing effort, other demands on her time made it impossible for her to continue. Nevertheless, everything in the final product has been shared with her.

We would also like to thank Diane Young for helping to edit the original draft and Linda Cerruti for serving as the copy editor of the final manuscript. The authors also want to express appreciation to the Community College League of California for sponsoring the publication of this document and to Rachel Rosenthal for providing the book cover photo.

1

External Funding and Regulations

VINEYARD SYMPOSIUM ISSUES

- Dealing with state and local revenue cuts.

  - Creating a "money-minded" culture.

  - Maintaining morale, innovation, and prosperity during tough budget times.

  - Using the budget crisis as a vehicle for positive change and as an opportunity to introduce creative solutions.

- Handling problems related to funding in both good and bad times.

  - Maximizing revenue when a college faces declining high school enrollments and a static population (or aging population) but must use a state funding model based on growth. At the same time, keeping

---

colleges from resorting to inappropriate practices as they have done in the past when faced with few growth options.

- Helping the college community understand why it is necessary to increase efficiency by increasing class size and eliminating unnecessary sections.

- Dealing with community demand for classes when a college is faced with limited resources to provide those classes because of changes in state regulations and priorities – particularly senior education, art classes, and physical education classes.

- Explaining necessary expenditures mandated by regulations that appear irrational to the college community when higher priority needs are not being met (e.g. FON (Faculty Obligation Number), 50% Rule, bond funds).

The CEO is the chief steward and, as such, manages and holds in trust the property, finances, and other affairs of the college, with ultimate responsibility for all matters. The chief steward role is probably tested most during difficult times when the CEO has to provide leadership to help the institution surmount challenges created by reductions in revenue.

California community colleges are publicly funded institutions dependent on the collection of state and local taxes. As such, they are susceptible to economic cycles and the resulting decreases/increases in tax revenue. One of the benefits to this relationship is that tax revenues generally lag economic changes by one year. That is, the tax revenues collected in 2016 are based on the economic activity of 2015. If colleges are diligent, they should always have at least a one-year warning of an increase or decrease in revenues. Unfortunately, and too often, colleges are passive and wait to make adjustments until they know the amount of the change in the year of the actual tax revenue collection. Critical attention needs to be paid to state and local economic information, so that a year in advance a college can prepare for a revenue reduction or begin to ramp up for a revenue increase and the inevitable funding of growth.

In preparing a college for a reduction in revenue and the resulting reduction in expenditures, the first step must be complete, financial transparency. Too often, CEOs (and CBOs (college business officers)) want to maintain "secret" pockets of money that can be used as emergency funds or "cushions." However, when discovered (or even suspected), it causes the college community to distrust the financial information being provided and to assume the financial problem is being overstated. Providing accurate and complete financial data with declared emergency funds or cushions is a much better strategy. There is no way to obtain employee involvement in finding financial solutions until they believe the numbers. Commitment to being financially transparent is a necessary but not a sufficient condition. The data must be understandable as well. Committing to financial transparency is a CEO decision and mandate, but making finances understandable requires teaching. Furthermore, financial transparency is a critical element to college leadership, whether it is during difficult financial times or periods of robust funding. Transparency is a cornerstone to building trust in the college leadership and is critical as a precursor to all financial discussions.

Ideally, during all financial presentations, but particularly during a revenue reduction situation, it is best if the CEO is the teacher for the college community. That means the CEO needs to understand how community colleges are funded, the nature and cause of the changes in revenue, and the effects on the college budget. Many CEOs do not have this working knowledge and always turn the presentation over to the CBO. While this honors the CBO and his or her knowledge, it undermines the leadership of the CEO because it looks like the CBO is in charge of resolving all financial matters. Also, because of the difference in backgrounds, the CEO is often the better teacher. As in the classroom, different approaches should be used when teaching employees about community college finances and the college budget. The most effective method may be to begin with small-group workshops for administrators, faculty leaders, and classified staff leaders. If done properly, the college would have a base of knowledgeable people who will be available to answer questions. This should be followed by open college forums in which people are free to ask questions. In all these teaching situations, it is best led by the CEO in concert with the CBO and the other senior leaders. Using this method not only educates the college community about community college finance and the college budget, but it should demonstrate that the CEO is running the organization with a well-coordinated team of senior executives, with each having knowledge in his or her area of responsibility. This secondary benefit helps to reassure the college community that the leadership of the college is in good hands and that any financial challenge will be handled successfully.

When leading these financial workshops, remember that everyone has different learning styles – especially when it comes to numbers. To be effective, presentations, at a minimum, will need to be a blend of numerical data, graphs, and narrative. Some people will want to see all the numbers, and they can be made available. Others will want a visualization of the situation, and a third group wants to be told what it all means. Since the goal is to have maximum understanding among members of the college community, do it all.

If the CEO does not have a solid, working knowledge of community college finance and the college budget, an unhealthy situation can be created because it makes the CEO vulnerable, and it is actually a disservice to the CBO. An organization is more effective if the CBO and CEO have an open dialog about college finances. Both the statewide CBO organization and the Chief Instructional Officers (CIO) organizations run training programs for new vice presidents. The CIO organization is particularly helpful in learning about FTES (Full-time Equivalent Student) calculation. However, they are both wonderful sources of information on community college finance and would surely welcome a CEO who would like to join the training.

Once the college has full disclosure of the financial data and understands the data, the college can begin to have a dialog about solutions without arguing about the accuracy of the numbers. This is an absolutely necessary first step. A college cannot wrestle with difficult solutions until everyone agrees on the definition of the problem and understands why that is an accurate description of the circumstances.

Incidentally, this financial transparency and the understanding of community college finance in California is equally helpful in good times. When the college community understands how the system works, people readily understand the necessity of certain strategies to maximize revenue, and they also understand the boundaries of what additional expenditures the college can undertake. Too often, in good times, the college community will overestimate the amount of new revenue available, and it will create equally unpleasant disagreements over decisions about new activities and new expenditures. Therefore, as part of transparency, include training on issues such as the state budget allocation process, budget cycles, growth funding, sustainability, FTES, FON, and reserves.

Financial transparency, teaching the employees of the college about community college finance in California, and helping people to fully understand the college budget are important parts of being an effective CEO and critical to dealing with a financial crisis. If CEOs are not teachers, they must become one. If they are not comfortable with finances, they need to gain enough knowledge so they are able to lead the activities described here. Success as a CEO depends on the ability to articulate the financial condition and needs of the college.

The next challenge for the CEO is to help the college deal with the reality of financial consequences of the downturn by moving past the emotional response. Understandably, most people's reaction is that the budget cuts to community colleges are unfair and unwise. People want to argue that community colleges are the least expensive form of higher education and should be protected during an economic downturn – particularly because community colleges provide the workforce training needed to stimulate the economy. The challenge for the CEO is to say, "You are right, but it is irrelevant to the task at hand." The college is having its revenue reduced and must cut expenditures even if it is unjust. However, there is a silver lining of sorts. When colleges face budget cuts because of reductions in state revenue, they are joined by every other community college. The challenge is not unique and is not aimed solely at one college. Furthermore, nobody at the college did anything wrong to cause the problem. Everyone can more easily move on with the task at hand when they are reminded this is a challenge shared with all their colleagues at other community colleges. If the aforementioned workshops have been conducted effectively, the employees understand what is happening in an economic downturn because information about budget reductions would have been part of the presentations mentioned previously. The situation is much more difficult when the revenue reduction is specific to a college and caused by previous decisions made by the college administration.

Once the aforementioned concerns have been accomplished, the CEO needs to lead the college in a collaborative modification of the budget to bring the budget in balance with the revenue reduction. The solution needs to be developed using representatives from each constituent group in the college (or district). The CEO needs to emphasize the shared responsibility and accountability expected of all employees. As part of this process, it is also important to help employees understand that a very large percentage of the budget is spent on total compensation to employees (especially explaining costs beyond gross pay). It will demonstrate the relatively small amount of discretion that is available to balance the budget beyond total employee compensation. At the same time, provide opportunities for employees to be creative by (1) having them participate in the development of cost-saving ideas (and use them); (2) asking for innovative ideas that are rewarded with a financial incentive (gift card, cash); and (3) funding their innovative ideas.

Because total employee compensation consumes such a large percentage of the budget, layoffs and cutbacks may be inevitable. First, don't publically plan layoffs with any specificity until it is absolutely certain that it is necessary. Unfortunately, the effect of layoffs is not felt evenly across the college because the greatest impact in layoffs is to permanent classified employees and part-time faculty. CEOs like to say it is not personal, and it is not from a CEO point of view but, to the affected person, it is highly personal. CEOs need to watch their language in these situations. These decisions can have an impact on entire families because the layoff is not only a loss of income but also a loss of family health benefits. If CEOs are not careful, they appear insensitive and lose "favor" as the CEO. Furthermore, letting people know there is a plan to lay them off, and then find it is not necessary, creates an irreconcilable personnel situation with those individuals and their colleagues. They will feel undervalued and that they will always be the first to go no matter how well they do their job. Second, if it is necessary, the CEO needs to be transparent with the process, be visible, be honest and be courageous. More specifically, for each layoff:

1. explain the budget situation;
2. treat affected employees with respect and dignity;
3. carefully consider the situation and timing in determining the time to inform individual employees – day of the week, time of day, and time of year (avoid actions before or after holidays);
4. follow established protocols;
5. consider unique opportunities;
6. consider early retirements or furloughs;
7. personally meet with affected individuals, units, and unions; and
8. allow for appeals.

Whenever CEOs get together, there is inevitably a discussion of college finance and budgets. However, at the Vineyard Symposium, accomplishing the actual task of developing and implementing a collaboratively created budget solution that balanced the budget was not the issue. CEOs seemed to have mastered the process of accomplishing that goal, so it will not be addressed further here (there are many other good sources of information on how to conduct such a process, and the purpose of this book is to focus on issues raised at the Vineyard Symposium). Rather, the issues that CEOs wanted to discuss at the symposium were how to engage the challenge of revenue reductions in a way that would still create positive outcomes for the college – in morale, innovation, positive changes, and creative solutions.

All CEOs should have a well-developed vision for their college, along with a strategy for achieving the vision, and one that has been embraced by the entire college community. When facing budget reductions, the CEO should be mindful of the opportunities being presented to achieve the vision. Often, many members of the faculty are wonderfully egalitarian and dislike cutting other people's programs. However, in the face of a budget problem, it is much easier to accomplish necessary reductions. Therefore, the CEO must use the opportunity to move the college toward the vision by making necessary cuts in programs, class offerings, services, and management that not only help solve the budget problem but also to make progress towards achieving the vision. For example, a number of colleges have used austere times to make changes in bookstore operations and food services. Don't ever take the politically expedient method of cutting everyone by the same percentage. Likewise, when the time comes to grow back, don't just replace what you cut, and don't let everyone grow by the same percentage. Grow in a manner that helps to achieve the vision.

A critical element in any downsizing of the college should be to serve the maximum student demand with the greatest efficiency. This is the opportune time to work on increasing average class size. Simply reducing the number of sections will accomplish that, but if it is done in a surgical manner the results can be much greater, and you can serve even more students. Every college needs to constantly monitor its average class size because it can be the biggest variable in expenditure control without jeopardizing revenue. During these periods of retraction, there is the least resistance because, by and large, everyone wants to serve as many students as possible while balancing the budget. The tougher part is when a college grows back, it must preserve the increased efficiency by being selective in the addition of new sections.

If the CEO has not developed a vision and/or the college has not collaborated on developing the vision, a budget crisis presents a wonderful time to create a collaborative vision. This may seem counterintuitive because the college is just trying to survive the cuts, but it reinforces the idea that all economic changes are cyclical and that the college needs to be ready for the next period of prosperity. It creates a feeling of optimism during the hard work of making the appropriate expenditure reductions. Even if a college has a developed vision, it may be helpful to revisit that vision in order to help the college keep its eye on the long term and not just focus on the short-term difficulties.

While it may seem to be an odd time to be working on accomplishing the vision for the college (beyond opportunistic reductions), it is important to remember that not all progress requires money. For example, it is a time in which the campus can mobilize to improve campus appearance through voluntary programs with employees, students, and community members. The same can be said for voluntary participation to improve outreach programs with administrators, faculty, and students working with feeder high schools, employers, and community groups. It is also a great time for the CEO and other executives, along with appropriate faculty, to build public-private partnerships and integrate them into the vision for the college. Even low-cost marketing efforts are possible (e.g. compiling student success data and stories, reproducing them on campus, and using them with outreach efforts at feeder high schools).

Most importantly, in tough budget times it is critical for people to know they are "cared for" and "cared about." The best way to demonstrate caring is through the continuation of professional development activities by the college, even if these activities cannot be retained in the same form. Develop a program that can be attended on campus or by webinar. Invite colleagues to speak on salient issues, such as enrollment management, technology in the classroom, equity and inclusion, etc. The point is to not be passive and victimized by the externally imposed budget cuts. The college needs to feel it is still in control and can make progress in spite of what has been imposed on it. For the CEO, whether speaking on campus or in the community, it is important to accurately describe the financial situation but to not take a position of "woe is me." Instead, deliver the message that the college will not be stopped and will continue to make progress while dealing with this temporary, economic down-cycle.

This attitude and philosophy is particularly important if the college is going to seek outside funds from donors and foundations. Donors want to give to winners or those with the prospect of being winners. They will usually not give funds to fix a financial problem, but they can be interested in funding innovation while you wrestle with the financial problems. The important element is to demonstrate that you are on track to being something special and that the current budget cuts will not be a deterrent in achieving the college's vision.

One final note on these state-imposed budget cuts. When the state is cutting revenue to the community colleges, there is a greater readiness to relax, modify, or remove rules and regulations. It is particularly true when those actions will allow for a pilot program or an experiment. The state will feel as if it is not a big gamble to allow rule exceptions if it is a small pilot program or experiment – particularly if it will create something innovative. The rule changes can even be temporary. Resistance to experiments and pilot programs is much less than to formal rule changes or permanent changes. In reality, every new idea is an experiment or pilot. If something doesn't work, there is no desire to keep doing it; and, if there is a better way of doing it, it will be changed. People at all levels are just more comfortable and less resistant to new ideas and approaches when they know the change is not permanent. Of course, if the experiment is successful, no one wants to go back! Remember, political leaders, just like foundations and donors, like to find ways to be positive and creative during financially difficult times and to be associated with winners and winning ideas. For example, it was during difficult financial times that Pierce College created new and creative partnerships with U.C. Berkeley and Caltech.

Funding Problems

Before responding to the specific funding issues, it is important to briefly discuss budget practices that should be consistently applied in both good and bad times.

1. Estimate revenue conservatively.
2. Develop a culture of planning where all requests are considered during annual budget development.
3. Manage year-end balances.
4. Establish a culture in which a conservative approach to district or college finances is the norm, and spend conservatively but fairly.
5. Develop values that include planning for an uncertain future.
6. Ensure policies and procedures are in place that require a prescribed level of reserves.
7. Ensure budget management procedures are in place for monitoring internal and external factors that could change budget assumptions.
8. Ensure flexibility in the event of unanticipated changes in revenue, expenses, or community needs.
9. Develop and share a budget plan.
10. Maintain a balanced budget.
11. Keep a stated budget cushion.
12. Have appropriate accountability, internal controls, and monitoring.
13. Provide sound instructions to finance and budget staff.

Develop a budget process that:

- is simple and easy to understand;
- provides for financial stability;

- provides for an appropriate level of reserves consistent with board policy and direction;
- is an integral part of the college planning process and related to goals and objectives;
- provides means to address any current or future emphasis directed by the board of trustees;
- promotes efficient use of college resources;
- allows flexibility for "local" control with accountability; and
- is planned in a multi-year cycle.

Growth

Except during difficult financial times, the state will always support some level of funded growth because of its desire to improve access. However, even though some level of funded growth is universally available, it does not mean every college is facing excess student demand. In some cases, colleges may be facing enrollment declines. The first critical area of examination is the feeder high schools. Headcount from feeder high schools is so important because these students are disproportionately represented in the college's full-time student population, and, as a result, have the greatest impact on FTES. The first effort should be to examine the capture rate of the high school graduation population in comparison to other community colleges. All colleges can benefit from increasing the capture rate; consequently, it is a good idea to maintain regular research on what changes need to occur to improve the rate. A complete understanding of why a college does not receive all graduates will direct the college to the remedies. Different strategies will be developed based on the results. Is the college losing students to neighboring community colleges or local, four-year universities? Why? Are students drawn to more attractive alternatives or avoiding the college or both? Is there a significant percentage of students who are not participating in higher education? Why? Is it for financial reasons or lack of interest in going to college or both? These are just examples, but the research will clearly help develop a strategy to increase high school graduation capture rates.

A second area of concern is an examination of whether the college is fulfilling its workforce development mandate. Has the college done a gap analysis to insure the educational programs are matched properly with labor demands? Does the college have meaningful partnerships with employers and a meaningful job placement operation? Again, research is needed to answer these and many other questions, but the results will drive the necessary strategies.

Similar analysis should be done for each programmatic segment and each demographic segment of the population served. Is each program adequately serving the intended purpose? Is the college offering the necessary educational programs and services to attract each demographic segment? Are there populations within the college's service area that are underrepresented in the college? If so, why are they not coming? The point here is to break down the analysis to ascertain what is needed to change decision making by potential students; and once that is learned, the strategy will be obvious. Examples of possible programmatic solutions include increased online education; prison education; concurrent enrollment; dual enrollment; home-schooled student enrollment; international student programs; veteran programs and services; community education (fee based); and contract education.

A college should be doing this type of research on an on-going basis so that the college is continually working or planning on how to build enrollment. Enrollment of new students is not simply a spigot that can be turned on and off based on the level of funded growth provided by the state. This is really the critical part of marketing. Too many people only think of marketing as the delivery of the message, but the really important part is to have an in-depth understanding of the college's service area and potential students within that area. That includes an understanding of: how people make education decisions, the educational needs of current and potential students, college image, etc.

The other side of the enrollment issue is retaining the students currently enrolled and helping them to be successful. If every college increased its retention rates among current enrollees and increased student persistence towards student goals, the college would increase enrollment and FTES. Furthermore, if a college increases student success, it will enhance the college's image and reputation and also attract more new students. This raises the issue of image and reputation. Certain colleges have developed such an exemplary reputation and image that they attract students from a much larger service area than just the one defined by district boundaries. These attractions may be real or simply perceived by potential students, but it has resulted in certain colleges having enrollments that far exceed normal draws from their primary service area. Image and reputation do matter and need to be attended to by a college. In addition to research, image and reputation need to be continually addressed because these perceptions are established over time and are not easily changed.

In some circumstances, there may be certain rules or regulations that prohibit the college from adequately serving a segment of the population (e.g. senior education or portions of dual enrollment). While not an easy or quick solution, efforts should be made to change the laws when the college feels the restrictions are wrong. At the same time, colleges can push the envelope created by the various rules and regulations but not cross the line. In many cases, overly restrictive rules were created because of abuses. Also, the consequences of having to return funds and having an adjustment in base FTES can haunt the college for a long time.

A college may need to consider one other alternative. The research results may indicate that, based on geographic boundaries, population characteristics, competition, etc., the college should be smaller in the long run. This is a useful, although painful, exercise. If research indicates the college should be within a smaller, specific size range, that range can be equated to a revenue estimate. Assuming you were starting from scratch, how would you build a great college within those revenue limits for that size of student population? Bigger is not necessarily better. How would you make being smaller an advantage? Would you be more focused on programs that better fit your population? Obviously, this type of change would be painful because it would indicate the discontinuance of programs, class offering reductions, and staffing reductions at all levels (including administrators), but it may indicate short-term change that would be helpful and give the college a long-term solution if it ever became necessary.

Average Class Size

Helping the college to understand why it is important to increase average class size requires a well-thought-out teaching experience. The college community does not understand the magnitude of the financial impact from these changes. The easiest way to teach this is to work through the consequences of a 10 percent increase in average class size. If it is assumed a college offers the same number of sections, but at a 10 percent increase in average class size, the college will generate 10 percent more FTES revenue without any increase in expenses. This is an incredible injection of new revenue, and the average class size probably only rose by less than four students. Frequently, colleges that are experiencing financial difficulties are also experiencing smaller average class sizes than comparable colleges. The use of that comparative data is an important part of the presentation.

In raising the average class size, the goal is to increase the number of students enrolled at census. The place to start is to make sure the schedule of classes matches student demand in terms of course offerings, facility utilization, time, coordination of course offerings, etc. The schedule needs to make student demand the priority – not faculty preference. The second effort needs to be retention or replacement of attrition between opening day and census. Efforts in this area include using waiting lists and first-week student appearances to replace no-shows and withdrawals. It also means faculty does not unnecessarily discourage students during the first week from taking the class. The third effort is the most obvious and that is to increase the maximum class size. However, that should not be done if it jeopardizes the educational integrity of the course. A college needs to recognize that the "burden" of increasing average class size falls on faculty, and the ability to make it happen requires the cooperation of the faculty. Therefore, it is imperative faculty understand the relationship of class size to job security, but it is also important that a portion of the savings is dedicated to an expenditure that provides a direct benefit to faculty.

Defunded Programs
When the state decides it can no longer fund certain programs, it is usually a result of a shortage of funds, isolated abuses (e.g. physical education), or a philosophical belief that the program needs to be supported by user fees and not state funds (e.g. senior education). It is not a condemnation of the merits of the program. However, at a minimum, these programs are being given a lower priority by the state, and such a declaration causes an immediate emotional reaction among the students in those programs as well as a justifiable fear among the students that their program will be discontinued.

Many students will simply accept the decision by the state. However, among other populations (e.g. seniors), that may not be the case. In dealing with these students, the CEO is faced with another teaching experience. CEOs need to clearly state they believe in the merits of the program (otherwise the college would have eliminated it at an earlier date) and that, if the resources are provided, the college will continue the program. The key is to help students understand this is not an adversarial situation between the students and the administration, but rather everyone is on the same side of the issue in opposition to the state. Start by clearly describing the actions of the state and the impact on the college. Then provide alternatives within the regulations (e.g. auditing, continuing education, contract education). Next, give the students a constructive course of action (e.g. mount a political effort to get the regulation changed, or find an alternative funding source). Finally, the CEO needs to convince the students (and believe it him/herself) that s/he and the students are in this together and need to work together in finding a solution because it is a clear case of an imposed decision from outside the college.

Irrational Rules and Regulations

It is easier to understand the existence of rules and regulations that appear irrational when one realizes the rules were created from a fundamental distrust of local boards that were allowed complete freedom in making expenditure decisions. In some cases, the distrust comes from the electorate (capital outlay bonds) or from faculty organizations and unions (FON, 50% Rule), but in all cases the distrust is, at a minimum, supported by the state legislature and/or board of governors who enacted the rules and regulations.

The first order of response is to fully explain the rule or regulation, its purpose, and its origin. Members of the community usually are unaware of the restrictions, which is also true for many members of the college community. It is also useful to explain the desire and the resistance to changing the rules in a manner that fairly represents both sides. Besides the rationale, the CEO should also explain the political realities and give a clear sense of the relatively small range of possible alterations in the laws.

While living in this world of apparent irrationality, it is useful for the CEO to inform the college community that a college does not know its actual revenue until the month of February, following the end of the fiscal year on the prior June 30. It is not a problem when a college has an unexpected windfall of extra revenue, but it can be a real problem to learn about a reduction in revenue nearly eight months after the last expenditure. A college is then forced to backfill the revenue reduction with current-year revenues. A CEO will gain great sympathy from the community (especially the business community) when they learn how hard it is to manage a budget when there is such a delay in reporting. It also underscores the need for reserves to handle this reporting problem when it is not possible to adjust expenditures. Of course, reserves are actually critical for many other reasons, but many people are unaware of this strange financial management problem confronting California community colleges.

2

Accreditation

VINEYARD SYMPOSIUM ISSUES

- Dealing with the problems created by accreditation becoming a continuous process that consumes excessive amounts of institutional energy. For example:

  - the drain on faculty and administrator time due to continual production of reports;

  - the drain on resources to redirect necessary staff to meet research requirements (especially in small colleges); and

  - the drain on morale from having to spend more time avoiding (or removing) sanctions than improving education.

- Exploring ways to reduce AACJC's (Accreditation Commission for Community and Junior Colleges) (Accreditation Commission) decision to more readily impose sanctions as an accreditation response.

Over the last 20 years, one of the most dramatic changes in the political environment for public community colleges has been the efforts by external agencies and legislatures to make community colleges more publicly accountable for student success. Previously, accountability was frequently defined by institutional effort with only a modicum of focus on student outcomes. The shift has been to make student outcomes (and the supporting data collection and analysis) the overwhelming accountability measure for colleges with the increased emphasis on student access, success, and completion. This shift has occurred at the national level as well as the state and local level. With this increased focus on student outcomes, colleges are now required to dramatically increase their research efforts to produce the required data. In some states, the move to accountability has infiltrated the area of finance by the adoption of performance-based funding.

This shift in higher education has made an impact on regional accreditation, especially in California. Historically, accreditation was designed to help colleges improve their operation and performance. In so doing, the accrediting commission was not operating as a compliance or enforcement agency and accordingly was not viewed as being punitive in nature. Sanctions against colleges were rare. Colleges were expected to be responsive to accrediting commission recommendations and, by and large, colleges were responsive. However, some people believed the process was not tough enough and that it allowed colleges to be too self-determinant in their operation and response to recommendations. There was also the belief by some that the process was based too much on narrative and lacking a basis of data and evidence.

In response to this accountability movement, the current demands for institutional reporting and the expectations for evidence-based decision making at the national, state, and local levels now require extensive college research operations. Reporting student outcomes and conducting institutional research have become standard operations. The reporting requirements are extensive and not limited to accreditation requirements. In California, state and Chancellor's Office requirements have called for a comprehensive and integrated assessment of student support services, student measures of success, programs of study, program review, curriculum review, as well as administrative operations assessments, climate studies, and more. The proliferation of state reporting added to the accrediting commission requirements of evidence and data-based performance of standards have increased considerably the research demands on colleges.

In addition to the aforementioned research requirements, the accrediting commission has also changed its method of operation (probably in response to the criticism that the process was too lax) to maintain an on-going relationship with its member colleges. The current accreditation requirements to submit regular written reports such as responses to accreditation recommendations, accreditation follow-up reports, and accreditation mid-term reports, even when accreditation is reaffirmed, has added to this burden on college human and fiscal resources. The increased reporting is exacerbated by the recognition that educators tend to be prolific writers. This is especially true when sanctions are handed down frequently and have a huge impact on the reputation of a college and enrollment and, therefore, finances. As a result, it is not unusual to have mid-term reports of 50 – 75 pages and self-study reports exceeding 200 pages, not counting the attached document evidence. One way to reduce the burden is to work with the commission to develop guidelines that will reduce the length of the reports without penalizing the colleges for brevity.

What the CEO Should Do
The accreditation process is required, a reality that is not going away – regardless of the angst that can be created by the requirements of accreditation. All employees must be supportive of the

process and understand its importance. The CEO is the lynchpin in how a college responds to accreditation. A few suggestions follow for the CEO.

1. Project a positive attitude and keep morale up about accreditation. Emphasize the importance of self-evaluation and continuous improvement for the college and the role these efforts play in the reputation of the college and success of students. Accreditation is the means to that end. Full accreditation is a must if the college is to render services and meet the needs of students.

2. Use established mechanisms to become more active with the Accreditation Commission in developing guidelines that will reduce the burden on the colleges and not result in penalties.

3. Establish systems and mechanisms to ensure the institutionalization of accreditation and a continuous focus on accreditation requirements so that reactions to accreditation are not "knee-jerk" but planned and ongoing. It may be necessary to have an accreditation liaison officer as a permanent position. This individual becomes the expert on accreditation and develops a plan with the involvement of others on activities for success in accreditation compliance.

4. Invest in a permanent research position or department because the function is needed for more than accreditation purposes.

5. Serve on accreditation visiting teams, and nominate or encourage staff to do so as well.

6. Provide training, through the accrediting commission, for board members and others.

7. Participate in training activities offered by the accrediting commission and others.

<u>Reform</u>

In recent years, reforming the accreditation process has been an important topic of conversation. If a college wishes to participate in reform efforts, this is an area that needs attention. Accreditation should not consume colleges so that the college cannot devote adequate time to educational reform. Perhaps this means redefining the purpose of accreditation and how it can be achieved within reasonable resource boundaries (both human and financial).

Effectively, the increased cost of accreditation is a "mandated cost" without recourse. No public community college can operate without being accredited; it is imperative that colleges comply with the dictates of its accrediting body. If it were a state agency making comparable requirements, a case could be made for the reimbursement of mandated costs. However, because the accrediting commission is an independent, member-supported agency, there is no place to go for cost recovery. Nevertheless, maybe the cost of accreditation should be factored into an increase in the base funding for colleges.

Accreditation for small colleges is an even bigger problem. The effort and resources necessary for data collection are not a function of college size. Therefore, a disproportionate burden is placed on small colleges in order to comply with the standards. Again, the reform effort needs to work on a solution that ranges from the state assuming a portion of the data collection effort (or provide funding to colleges or creating consortia) to changing the standards. To a lesser extent, but still significant, the other aspects of accreditation also create a greater burden for small colleges because they have a smaller work force to assume the responsibilities. Accreditation needs to be a factor when a community or a district is creating a college as opposed to having an educational center operating under the auspices of another college. There is great pride in having an independently accredited college, but sometimes the burdens exceed the value (not to mention some of the financial problems facing an independent, small college). There may need to be a critical mass of financial and human resources before a college becomes an independent institution.

Accreditation in higher education has received a great deal of attention in recent years. The Department of Education has become more involved. Alternatively, there is a view that regional accrediting commissions place undue burdens on colleges. Having said that, colleges need to recognize two distinct paths. One path is to work with state agencies and the accrediting commission to reform the process; but more importantly, until it changes, a college must live with the reality of the current process. That means the college needs to be prepared to interact with the accrediting body in a manner that demonstrates compliance with the existing standards, data, internal processes, etc. to maintain accredited status. This distinction is important because it will not do a college any good to be bogged down in discussions about the perceived injustices of the current practice when there is so much work to be done to conform to the requirements. If the college wants to simultaneously participate in reform efforts, that should be an effort separate and apart from the compliance process.

Any discussion about reform needs to begin with a dialog about the purpose of the current data and evidence collection for both the accrediting body and state agencies. Is there a fundamental distrust of locally controlled colleges to do the right thing so that their performance must be monitored? Is there really a belief that colleges have not cared about student outcomes and student success until these reporting requirements were instituted? How does the system develop equitable and appropriate benchmarks for the data to insure differences among the colleges are reflected and inappropriate comparisons between colleges are avoided? To what end will all the data be used? Does the system wish to punish "poor" performers and/or reward "superior" performers? In what way is all the collected data being used to improve student success? Given all the human and financial resources being used to comply with state and accreditation reporting requirements, is the system confident that it generates the desired improvements? What is being sacrificed by these reporting requirements? Could those resources be better used to directly improve student success? Are all the colleges suffering because of the actions of a few colleges? There are many more questions, but perhaps an assessment of current practices can take place that leads to a more successfully designed future.

Probably the biggest part of the accreditation controversy revolves around the increased use of sanctions imposed by the Commission on colleges. It makes the process more adversarial and punitive which is very different from the process of 20 years ago. On the one hand, it can be argued that, without sanctions, certain colleges routinely ignored recommendations, and the sanctions were necessary to demonstrate this behavior was unacceptable. The opposing view is that sanctions are very damaging to an institution and frequently have nothing to do with the academic integrity of the college (e.g. Board of Trustee behavior). It is also not clear where the boundaries are between the state chancellor being responsible to reform a college and where the responsibility falls to the accrediting body. College finances are a classic example of this dilemma. Reform needs to determine these distinctions in the form of a delineation of function and to see if there is a more acceptable sanction process.

3

Building Trust

```
┌─────────────────────────────────────────────┐
│          VINEYARD SYMPOSIUM ISSUES            │
│                                               │
│  •  Establishing that the first step in       │
│     leadership development is an authentic     │
│     self-assessment.                           │
│                                               │
│     •  Making oneself open to critical         │
│        analysis by others.                     │
│                                               │
│     •  Learning to continually reflect on      │
│        one's own leadership performance.       │
│                                               │
│  •  Building relationships of trust between    │
│     employees and administrators,              │
│     particularly with a relatively new CEO.    │
│                                               │
│  •  Forming strategies for building trust      │
│     within different institutional             │
│     circumstances.                             │
│                                               │
│     •  A college history of extensive          │
│        administrative turnover has created     │
│        an environment lacking continuity       │
│        and trust.                              │
└─────────────────────────────────────────────┘
```

- Significant abuses of trust occurred by previous leaders.

- Lack of trust among members of the administrative team.

- A vacuum created by a weak chancellor or president so everyone went directly to the board and the board micromanages. No one trusts the defined processes and, yet, is afraid to stop dealing directly with board members.

- Recovering from having to make tough decisions before the CEO could create an environment of trust.

Developing one's own leadership abilities can be a dilemma. In part, leadership ability is very personal because it must be derived from one's personality and unique characteristics. It is also a consequence of each person's life and leadership experiences. At the same time, a set of leadership skills that is common to all leaders must be internalized in order to become an effective leader. That process begins with an authentic self-assessment of one's strengths and weaknesses. It may also require input from others (particularly a coach or mentor) because no CEO sees a clear picture looking in the mirror. A leader must also continue to learn and reflect on his or her leadership because it is an ability that needs to continue to grow and evolve throughout one's career and life. That means a CEO must keep learning about new leadership techniques, slowly integrate the new leadership skills into his/her leadership performance, evaluate that performance, and make any necessary changes. There is no magic wand. Leadership development is a continuous process of learning, applying, reflecting, and correcting. It is a never-ending process; all exceptional leaders were still growing and developing on their last day of leadership.

Building Trust

Trust is defined as the "firm belief in the reliability, truth, ability, or strength of someone or something." It is a key ingredient in the success of any relationship, especially between CEOs and anyone with whom the CEOs becomes involved with in the course of their work (a board, community members, and college constituent group members). Creating trust between leaders and their constituents is always unique to each leader. Trust is person specific. The environment that preceded a CEO only determines how long or how hard a leader needs to work to create the trust; it does not predetermine the outcome. If a CEO inherits a culture of trust, people expect that to be the normal relationship and it should be easier to obtain it, provided the new CEO is worthy of trust. If a CEO inherits a culture of distrust, it may take a greater effort to develop it, but the bond with the leader will be stronger and the trust will be deeper because constituents see it in the context of a leader's predecessors. Also, no CEO assumes office with a relationship of trust already established. Even inside candidates must develop trust as a CEO; it is not automatically generalized from the former position (e.g. vice president). The CEO position is entirely new, and, like anyone else, the CEO must earn the trust.

No effective leader can operate without trust, so it may be the most critical ingredient in being a successful leader. Yet, it is attainable by every CEO. Even authoritarian leaders (e.g. military leaders) need the trust of their followers at least to the extent that the followers believe the leader knows what he or she is doing and trust the judgment of the leader. In all situations, the trust must be reciprocal. It is not possible to create a long-term relationship of trust if leaders don't also trust their followers to perform their jobs and to act responsibly.

No one trusts incompetent leaders. Competency is determined by the actions of leaders, more than their words. That is why it is so important for CEOs to learn management skills as well as leadership skills. Learning and demonstrating that the CEO is a competent manager is the first step in becoming a trusted leader. However, remember it is only the first step. Managerial competency is a necessary but not a sufficient condition to being a trusted leader. There are many very competent managers who are either not trusted and/or do not evolve into being a leader.

The CEO must be knowledgeable. An essential element in gaining legitimacy which leads to trust is by demonstrating through word and deed the CEO has the knowledge required to move an institution forward. People need to know that the CEO possesses critical knowledge and then can apply that knowledge in ways that benefit the institution. For example, not only should CEOs be able to articulate the history and purpose of community colleges in general but must also be knowledgeable of the distinct history, mission, and values of their college. This knowledge, whether shared in written or spoken form, demonstrates the CEO has taken the time to learn the organization and cares about its history in the context of the present and in planning for the future. People want the CEO to be knowledgeable of the many aspects of the job. They also expect CEOs to be honest about what they do not know. Feigning knowledge where there is none, as well as not obtaining knowledge in areas of weakness, will definitely result in distrust.

Trust is built on respect as compared to liking you as a person. CEOs want people to be attracted to them as a leader, but it should not be an attraction based on popularity or friendship. The CEO emerges as a leader and creates trust by building relationships with people in the organization, not friendships. This is an important distinction and one that some CEOs have struggled with in the past.

People within the organization need to feel the CEO's position of leadership is legitimate. This is most often a problem when the selection process was short-circuited. Selection processes are not pleasant, and it is always tempting if a person is offered a position without going through the entire process. However, in the end, it is not helpful. People will feel that a CEO may not have been the best qualified or only was given the job because of some favoritism. It is hard enough being a trusted CEO without starting the job with a perceived liability among the people within the organization.

Listen

Too often CEOs feel that trust is created by what they say, instead of what they do. However, before taking action, a leader must learn to be a good and authentic listener. Listening is the great, underestimated talent. Everyone thinks they can listen and do listen, but authentic listening requires a conscious effort, concentration, and patience. Authentic listeners are not just going through the motions but are listening because they care what the other person has to say and want to understand the other person's message. To quote Steven Covey, "Most people do not listen with the intent to understand. Most people listen with the intent to reply." Listening is so effective because people trust people who listen to them. Genuine listening validates an individual and demonstrates caring for that person. Nothing does a better job of telling individuals they matter than listening to what they have to say. It builds enormous trust when people feel they have been heard. As Maya Angelou said, "I've learned people will forget what you said, people will forget what you did, but people will never forget how you made them feel." Authentic listening to other people makes them feel good about themselves, makes them feel important and, as a result, it helps them to trust you.

Part of effective listening is to talk and listen to as many people as possible – both inside and outside the organization, in agreement with you and in opposition to you. That means that part of being an effective listener is to avoid being defensive because it is important to hear and understand the opposition. It is particularly important to hear false perceptions because they can be among the easiest remedies. However, sometimes it is best to resist correcting every misperception at the time you hear it. It is frequently more effective to come back to it at a later time so you avoid what appears to be a defensive or argumentative comment. Also, the correction may require an action that is broader than communicating with a single individual. Furthermore, when leaders listen carefully to people, they can begin to understand a person's motivation and goals beyond the actual words being expressed. This level of understanding is a critical element in finding optimal solutions to problems and new ventures.

Listening can be the most difficult when the CEO is leading a group discussion, particularly in a participative governance situation. It is important to approach these situations without a predetermined solution the CEO is trying to sell to the group. If that is the case, just announce it rather than having the charade of participation. Also, this is where the CEO is not listening but forming a reply to further sell the predetermined solution. At the same time, the CEO must approach the situation with parameters for solutions or alternative solutions. To work properly, the CEO must trust the group (just as he or she wants to be trusted by the group) and listen to the input. It may produce a better solution or modify a solution by having real participation with a CEO who is listening to the group's contributions. The CEO should not try to control the group but instead provide the leadership that keeps the group from getting out of control. This concept underscores the importance of trust being reciprocal. Often, CEOs want the college community to trust them, but they don't trust the college community.

It does not take long for those feelings to be recognized and to create an environment of distrust – the opposite of the desired goal. Likewise, the CEO must be transparent. Withholding information or data demonstrates a lack of trust in the process, a lack of trust in the judgment or ability of the people within the organization, and a lack of reciprocity.

When CEOs are talking with other people within the college, they will usually be the more powerful person in the conversation. As a result, the CEOs will be more effective if they are the dominant listener and not the dominant talker. Listening is often not thought of in terms of power distinctions, but it is another important attribute to effective, active listening.

Beyond the direct benefit of establishing trust by listening, developing a college environment in which the leadership listens to members of the college community also creates a welcoming climate in which new ideas are embraced. Everyone in the college has ideas, and everyone has at least one really good idea. When people feel they will be heard, they are willing to come forward with their idea. Besides convincing people they will be heard, they must also be assured that they will not be humiliated. Therefore, it is important to listen to all the ideas and, if possible, find a way to support at least an element within the suggestion. If not, explain why it cannot be done but encourage the next idea. The goal is to try to create a college that tries to say "yes" rather than "no." If you do, it generates a spirit of everyone being part of the college and working to make it better, and the CEO will get a lot of great ideas. There is also an added trust benefit when a leader embraces a person's idea or suggestion.

Be Positive
People more readily trust a leader who is positive and instills hope and optimism. However, that optimism cannot be Pollyannaish. The optimism must have credibility and a planned path for achieving the desired future. This is particularly important when an

organization is struggling. It is easy for people to become hopeless and to withdraw into minimum organizational involvement. Yet, if the CEO can provide a valid sense of hope, people will respond. When people have hope for a better state of affairs, they will work extremely hard to make it happen.

Part of instilling hope and optimism is to create a positive feeling within the organization. Amazingly, the easiest way to create a positive environment and trust is to stop the negative behavior. That needs to begin with the CEO. Avoid berating others – especially your predecessor. Some CEOs feel they are competing with the people they succeeded and try to point out their shortcomings. Nothing is gained from doing this, and the supporters of the previous CEO will then be alienated. Actually, if CEOs are trying to build trust, they should be in the habit of not speaking negatively about other people. If the CEO berates others, people will assume the CEO will berate them behind their back and, therefore, not trust the CEO. Consistent with this axiom is that the CEO should avoid blaming others for the current state of affairs (e.g. the state, the district in multi-college districts) and should not revisit past wrongdoings by others. The whole point of creating a positive organization is to help the organization assume responsibility for their present state and work to take control of their future. Don't let the organization start to feel like a victim with no control. A positive leader will show how to move forward and achieve the organizational goals which, in turn, will create trust in the leader. Trusted leaders also take responsibility for their actions and assume accountability for their organizations as part of demonstrating control of an organization's destiny.

What starts to become apparent is that trust is created by demonstrating an array of specific leadership skills. There is no singular act or skill that creates trust between an organization and its leader. It is an entire collection of skills. To that end, there is available a series of additional leadership skills and characteristics that help build trust.

Be Authentic

People trust genuine people and don't trust chameleons and con artists. Don't be a different person in different settings. Leadership is more comfortable when it is a true manifestation of the person, and it builds trust when people feel they see the real person.

Earn Respect

CEOs gain enormous trust by demonstrating personal virtues (honesty, integrity, thoughtfulness, intelligence) in everything they do. One of the realities of being a leader is that people are always watching their leaders and judging them (even waiting in line for coffee). A leader is always on stage. Trust develops when people see these virtues being exhibited – particularly when leaders do not think they are being watched.

Keep Your Ego in Check

The egos and identities of leaders need to be separate from their jobs. Leaders need to avoid being self-promoters and unnecessarily making themselves the center of attention. When a leader is perceived to be a self-promoter, followers always worry that when things go wrong, the leader will "throw them under the bus." It is hard to trust a leader when that is the perception. Instead, as the leader, take responsibility for the organization and let organization successes be your promotion.

If leaders can separate their identity from their job, it is easier to listen to opposite opinions and ideas. Leaders gain trust by demonstrating they are not threatened by opposing ideas because they are always working to find the best solution and not just promoting the solution they developed. With that frame of mind, when people express thoughts different from the leader's thoughts, the leader is not defensive because it is not perceived as an attack on the leader's identity.

Trust is Personal and Relationship Based

In the end, when a college trusts its leader, it is the aggregate feeling of each individual trusting the leader. That is important to remember because ideally leaders connect with each person, or at least each person develops a sense of trust based on what others have told him or her based on their connection with the leader. It is easy for leaders to become so caught up in "leadership skills" that they forget that leadership is relationship based. Usually that relationship is through personal interaction or through feeling a connection when listening to a leader speak.

The personal connection begins with the CEO caring about people as individuals. In particular, make sure the people who are the CEO's direct reports know the CEO cares about them. Care about their well-being and personal challenges, but the caring should not extend to becoming friends with them. Not only should the CEO's direct reports know he or she cares about them but so should the entire college community. Communicate care and concern for the workforce in messaging by sharing ways in which you want to improve their work environment, salaries, and other critical aspects of their jobs. It is to this same end that it is important for CEOs to leave their office and walk around the campus so that they meet people in their own space. Make it a point to know the names of as many people as possible. There is no better way to make a personal connection than to call a person by name. Again, because leadership and trust are relationship based, try to demonstrate genuine caring about people as individuals in whatever way fits your personality. Even keeping the door open to your office helps because it encourages these casual interactions which all help to build a personal connection.

The other major means of a CEO building a personal connection is through public speaking. Sometimes the CEO becomes so focused on the substance of the primary message that the small things are forgotten. Hopefully, because the expression genuinely reflects the feelings of the CEO, it is important to use "we" instead of "I" and to show that the college is about "us" and not "me." The primary message is still a critical part of the speech, but the language the message is wrapped in will determine whether or not it also personally connects the leader with the audience.

Of course, substantive communication is a critical element in building and maintaining trust. The communication needs to be done frequently, accurately, and in a transparent manner by the CEO and not by others on behalf of the CEO. People need to know and hear the voice of the CEO. A college environment cannot generate a sense of trust without good communication. Ironically, it is hard to have communications heard and believed without trust. That is why frequency and transparency are important in communication and trust because they grow together.

Trust is a Marathon
Development of trust between a CEO and the college community occurs over an extended period through consistent actions, as described above, by the CEO. How long it will take depends in part on the environment inherited by the CEO when he or she assumes the position. Unfortunately, it takes time and effort to develop trust, and trust can be lost by a single act that violates that trust.

The other important element of building trust is that it must be reciprocal. Even though there is a power differential between a CEO and the college community, it is like all relationship-based connections, there must be mutual benefit and mutual trust to make the relationship last.

Trust in a Process
Processes will not be trusted unless the individuals involved are trusted. When a board of trustees micromanages around the CEO (a chancellor in a multi-college district and a president in a

single-college district), the micromanaging can only be stopped by the CEO. This type of behavior undermines trust in the CEO because the message is that he or she is irrelevant. In such a case, the board and the CEO are not properly assuming their roles. If the CEO is unable to train the board to be a policy board, then outside resources should be used to perform the training. At the same time, the CEO needs to assume operating responsibility for the district within the board-established policy parameters. If the CEO is unsure how to do this, a coach for the CEO should be engaged. When all parties assume their proper roles (the board stops people from going around the CEO and stops micromanaging), trust in the process will be restored. In multi-college environments, the same principle applies: the chancellor should not micromanage around a college president. There needs to be a relationship of trust and honesty between the two leaders. When issues of any kind come directly to the chancellor about a college situation, the chancellor must redirect those issues to the college president and allow them to take the natural course, and if necessary, for them to return to the chancellor's level. As in the case of the board, training may be required if the problem persists.

Recovering Trust

If a person is forced to make difficult decisions (budget cuts, layoffs, terminations) before building a trust relationship with constituents, two elements must be used in the decision-making process. First, complete transparency must be provided. The leader should not blame others (the chancellor or the board is making you do it) but instead provide all the information possible which explains why the decisions are necessary. As discussed earlier in Chapter One, if the CEO does not have a trust relationship, it is helpful to engage others who do have a trust relationship to help explain the circumstances. Second, the CEO must fully use participative management techniques so that constituents (or their representatives) feel involved. If this is done effectively, it will also produce speakers in the aforementioned transparency discussions. If the CEO has already made the decisions without adequate transparency or involvement, he or she has created a very difficult situation because the CEO must now reverse the distrust created before the CEO can build a trust relationship. The only solution is to "fall on your sword." The CEO must admit his or her mistakes, admit that inexperience led to an improper course of action, and give specific plans for how it will be different in the future.

Obtaining trust within an organization takes time; it does not develop with one action but through a series of actions over time. It can take years to develop trust, but it can be diminished with one action or sentence in a matter of seconds. Obtaining and sustaining trust makes a huge difference in leadership. CEOs must make sure to surround themselves with people of good character – people they trust and who will give them constructive criticism that makes them a better, more trustworthy leader.

4

Changing College Culture

VINEYARD SYMPOSIUM ISSUES

- Changing the style and method of operating a college when a CEO's predecessor was at the college a long time and everyone is used to that way of doing things.

- Changing a college culture that is rooted in the past and where power has been given to people invested in maintaining the status quo.

- Responding when people within the college say they want change but fight the solutions.

  - Employees say they don't want an autocratic president, but they are upset when you won't make decisions for them.

  - Faculty don't want to give up teaching the classes they have always taught and don't want to change the way they have always taught them.

- Senior employees take the call for change as a criticism.

- People don't want to do the work required for successful change.

- Sometimes faculty support change, but the deans resist it.

- The faculty feels entitled to more compensation and won't do anything new without being paid.

- Gaining a commitment to a new, shared vision when, due to college history, there has been no consistent plan or vision. If there were plans, employees don't believe those plans have meaning because the college has always simply ignored them.

  - How to overcome employee apathy – this is just another plan or vision for accreditation compliance by another leader.

  - Faculty are isolated from reality and what is happening outside the college but don't recognize it as a problem.

    - Faculty believe they are the best faculty in the country so don't see the need to explore alternatives.

    - Some faculty are even isolated within the college – they just live in their own department or area.

  - How does a small college gain more involvement and motivate employees when they already feel overburdened and burnt out?

- Changing a culture of incivility – for its own sake but also as a barrier to implementing other changes. In particular, concern for:

  - disruptive behavior and verbal bullying;

  - spreading false rumors; and

  - immoral and unethical behavior.

- Preparing college leaders as agents of change.

  - Many administrators are good managers but poor leaders. They don't know how to lead change so actually resist it.

  - How to help the people within the college cope with change?

    - Fear of the unknown

    - Seeing people being held accountable and removed when necessary.

    - Fear they are next.

The culture of a college defines the fabric of the institution. More specifically, culture refers to those things that are shared within the college community: shared knowledge and beliefs, shared values, shared behavioral expectations, and principles that are widely used or recognized. Changing the culture of an institution is probably one of the most challenging tasks a CEO can undertake. The challenge of changing the college culture must be approached with certain realities in mind: (1) the culture of the institution was years in the making and, in most cases, will not be changed in a short period of time; (2) changing the culture requires support from the CEO's supervisor and the board (or the chancellor, if appropriate); and (3) such a task should not be undertaken without careful planning and an understanding of the risks involved. The CEO, especially if he or she is new, needs to be clear about the mandate for change. Who determined the culture needs to change? Is the mandate for change the CEO's idea? Is it the board or chancellor (in a multi-college district) directing the new CEO to change the culture? Is the change movement the result of an accreditation recommendation? Does the CEO support the notion that the culture needs to change? The answers to these questions will determine the initial actions to be taken in the change process.

The new CEO, who has accepted a position with the mandate to change the culture, must learn as much about the institution as possible while simultaneously building relationships of trust with employees. Do not take any actions to change the culture in the first months or maybe even the first year. Learn and assess first. Let the board or chancellor know what the plan is so they will know what to expect: that change will not occur immediately, and when it does occur, there may be resistance. Change takes time.

The process for changing the culture of a college is a function of the relationship between the institution and its leaders, particularly the CEO. Accurately assessing the situation at the college and building positive relationships with the college community are necessary to yield favorable results. Irrespective of the culture and environment inherited from one's predecessor, leaders cannot effectively change the culture of the college without first establishing trust. While rules can be changed, the culture cannot be changed until people trust the leaders (see Chapter 3). This is particularly true if the college has had poor leadership experiences in the past, is vested in the status quo, or doesn't believe that planning matters. The CEO must first establish a trust relationship with the college community so he or she can lead willful followers and not just lead by the power of the position.

The accurate assessment of the college will aid in determining whether the current culture is positive or negative. Positive cultures may more readily trust a new leader but may be more resistant to change. When college employees perceive the college is doing well, they may not see any need to do things differently. That means the CEO will need to show a college how they can be even better. Colleges with negative cultures may be slow to trust a new leader, but when they do, they may actively embrace change. When college employees recognize the college is not doing well, they readily accept the idea of change. However, they may not yet believe the CEO is the right person to lead them in that effort because they have survived the lack of quality leadership and failed efforts in the past. The process of getting to know people, the college, and its customs will help to build confidence in the CEO.

Once trust has begun to be established and an assessment has been made, the critical next step is to create a shared vision of where to take the college. Don't talk about change or culture. Talk about what everyone wants the college to look like in the future based on your assessment (presumably they want a college that has a different culture). Using the word "change" makes people defensive because it implies there is something wrong with how things have operated in the past. This is a particularly sensitive issue to some long-term employees of the college. Instead, talk about going forward from the present to the future without reference to the past. This is also the time for the CEO to talk about the college accepting responsibility for its future and not relying on or blaming others. Creating the vision is the first step in a college taking control of its future.

Collaboratively developing a vision for the college and leading the college in the implementation of the vision is one of the most important challenges for a CEO. Successful completion of this endeavor is one of the institutional activities that truly establishes the CEO as the leader and ensures the college is moving in the right direction. Because of its importance, it is best if the CEO leads the process. If CEOs do not feel they have the skill set to effectively lead the creation of a collaboratively developed vision, they should use outside resources to help make it happen. However, the CEO cannot delegate the leadership for the implementation of the vision.

People more willingly accept change that is self-initiated and resist change that is imposed on them. Frequently, the impetus for change may come from outside the college (e.g. an accreditation recommendation or a board directive). However, externally initiated calls for change in the college culture won't actually be internalized by the college community until people within the college feel the change is rational and the appropriate direction for the college. That is why it is important to build a collaborative vision which is based on data and linear reasoning, even if the directive came from outside the college. If people can follow the logic of the vision, they will suggest improvements and eventually adopt a vision that will feel self-initiated. To achieve this feeling it is important for the CEO to be a teacher in the development of the vision. Share the relevant data and explain why the suggested elements of the vision are the appropriate directions for the college based on the data. The goal in the collaboration is to improve the vision and to help others understand the data and logic that is behind the development of the vision. This is an important distinction from selling the vision or blaming an external entity for the change. Remember, like all teaching situations, everyone learns differently and needs different methods to understand the issues and the solutions. Some members of the college community want to review all the data, while others want a narrative description, and still others want it represented visually. The CEO also needs to emphasize that visionary leadership may be the responsibility of the CEO, but the successful development and implementation of the vision is the responsibility of the entire college.

Presumably, the process of building trust and conducting an assessment has involved extensive, authentic listening, and, as such, the CEO should have a fairly complete sense of the qualities a vision must contain to gather support from employees and trustees. While the vision should not be completely composed of these elements, by including as many as possible, it will be an easier task to gain support from the college community and also demonstrate the CEO has been listening. From the "listening tour," the CEO should have a clear sense of the stakeholders, the issues within the institution, the changes everyone supports, and the pockets of resistance to any change.

In general, the vision should have components for the following:

1. making the organization distinctive and uniquely better;
2. solving the organization's problems;
3. increasing student success;
4. maintaining financial solvency while being a progressive and innovative college;
5. building from the organization's strategic advantages;
6. explaining how participation will occur (both method and style) and how decisions will be made (both process and communication);
7. pressing the envelope to embrace innovation;
8. presenting concepts and ideas that embrace the CEO's passion and the passions of as many people within the organization as possible; and
9. providing an overall tone that gives a positive and optimistic vision of the future.

The vision has to be taught by making everyone comfortable with why the various components are important to the college. For example, why raising the average class size is critical to generating monies to fund elements of the vision, and why that can only happen by changing the schedule of classes. Or, why the college can only increase student success by being responsive to student demands for classes. Or, why the college can only increase student success by exploring alternative ways of teaching and learning. Or, why the college must invest heavily in professional development so that employees will have the skills, knowledge, and abilities they need to fulfill the new vision.

The CEO must continually demonstrate the vision is driving decision making. Elements of the vision should be continually referenced and incorporated in decisions. A vision only has meaning when the leaders demonstrate it has meaning.

Employees want to be part of a great college, and leaders must convince them that accomplishing the vision will make the college a better place for students and a better place to work. Most importantly, the vision must contain the passion of the CEO so that the vision is communicated with passion. People must feel that passion and embrace that drive which, in turn, gets them to buy in and work to achieve the vision – even without additional pay. That commitment is even easier to obtain if the vision has also embraced the passions of employees. Doing things differently than the way they were done in the past undoubtedly means more work. Extra work is often the source of resistance. It is always easier to just continue operating the college the way it has always operated. Unless the CEO can gain the commitment of employees to the vision, it is hard to gain commitment to operating in a different way.

Collaboratively developing a vision and gaining the commitment of the college community to achieve the vision requires a skilled and talented leader. It means that all the aforementioned techniques need to be used but also that the CEO has a leadership relationship with the employees of the college. The employees must trust and believe in the leader in order for them to work to implement the vision. When CEOs reflect on great college leaders they have known, what sets them apart? It is the ability to collaboratively lead the development of a creative, meaningful vision but more importantly to have the leadership relationship with the college community to gain their support to make the vision a reality.

Too often, people make the mistake of confusing the leadership of a college with being a great orator or having the charisma of a celebrity. There is only one Martin Luther King, Jr. and only one John Kennedy but an enormous number of great leaders who lack either of these unique abilities and characteristics. What a college leader is striving to achieve is a relationship with the college community in which people feel connected to the leader, are excited by the leader's ideas, are enthusiastic about the direction of the college, and feel a sense of loyalty to the leader. The key to achieving this relationship is for leaders to find their unique path that is a function of their personality and abilities. It is a collection of many attributes, as described in any good book on leadership, and fitting those attributes to the unique circumstances of the college and the unique personality of the leader. Those attributes range from being intelligent, accessible, caring, humorous, and organized to being hard working, optimistic, logical, honest, and prepared. It is the collection of attributes that are special, not just having any one of them. Most importantly, it is how those attributes create a special relationship with the college community. Once established, the relationship invests in the leader the power to achieve the vision through leading a collaborative effort of the institution.

Even under the best of circumstances, there can be legal barriers. The most difficult part of creating a new culture is overcoming these barriers, particularly contractual barriers. Unfortunately, some colleges have surrendered management rights to employee groups through negotiated contracts (for example, a faculty contract that stipulates that course and class offerings and cancellations are exclusively within the domain of elected faculty chairs). One solution is to attach financial incentives to average class sizes above established criteria. Chairs may be willing to make the difficult decisions to achieve those incentives for their department or be willing to surrender the authority to the dean to capture the incentives. In this situation, either the provision must be negotiated away or alternative behavior incentivized to create the desired outcome within the existing contract.

It is not enough to talk about change and create documents that describe what the future touted in the vision looks like. Actions must be taken and commitments made simultaneously so that employees know the CEO and the board of trustees are committed to realizing the vision for the success of students. An investment in professional development and innovation is key to bringing change to an organization. As part of the vision (or its implementation), develop an organization that tries to say "yes" and embraces new ideas. Also, develop a process for funding and assessing the impact of new ideas once they have been funded. Try to create an atmosphere that is excited about new and different ways of doing things. Everyone has an idea of how to improve their work – help employees make it a reality by providing support for implementation. Another way to stimulate that thinking is to create interdisciplinary interactions on campus so that employees learn about other parts of the campus and explore new interdisciplinary partnerships. Also, a college can stimulate new ideas by sending groups to other innovative colleges within California and beyond. Make it possible for employees to participate in such endeavors.

Provide professional development activities for managers and others in the organization so that they know their appropriate role in and understand the change initiative. Don't assume all leaders within the organization are capable of leading and managing change. Moving the college in a new direction involves taking risks (some ideas will fail) and hearing ridicule ("that will never work"). Remember, maintaining the status quo is the safest path and the one of least resistance. However, status quo will also cause the organization to stagnate and slip into mediocrity or worse. Leaders must protect people who take risks (e.g. take the blame for them) and learn how to insulate themselves from the fears and ridicule of instituting change.

A vibrant college needs to have professional development workshops that focus on being a leader as well as a good manager. Too often, colleges focus on developing managerial skills within managers, which is important, but developing leadership skills may be even more important and more difficult. It is helpful to the organization if these workshops are not exclusive to managers but also include faculty and classified leaders. Developing institutional leadership skills helps to build a leadership team that cuts across all employee segments and has everyone working toward a common vision. Many important people within the college may want to provide leadership, but don't know how, and want to help people having difficulty dealing with change, but don't have the skills to assist them. Giving them those skills will help them to grow and to achieve the vision.

Resistance to new ideas and new directions is not necessarily obstinacy or a fear of more work. For people who thrive on certainty and control, change can be threatening, particularly because it may mean surrendering control to others. Having professional development workshops that provide skills for helping these individuals can increase the success of the effort.

When implementing change and elements of the vision, start with the ones that have broad-based support. Always start, if possible, with little wins. Build on those wins. Also, if it is possible to implement changes in part of the college first, find the largest unit in the organization that believes in the change and has the leadership to make the change and start with them. Success breeds success by allowing others to see the benefits of change, while also reducing anxiety about the consequences of the change by seeing that it can occur without experiencing any significant problems.

In very difficult environments, the vision process may need to be divided into two parts. First, develop a short-term vision in which a series of small wins can be accomplished. This should help build institutional confidence in the leadership of the CEO. Second, once the short-term vision has been achieved, tackle the long-term vision that addresses the culture of the college and the larger institutional efforts.

The civility issue is part of the vision but needs to be handled in a different manner. It needs to become a value of the organization that starts at the top. First, trustees must embrace it and demand it as part of the decorum of board meetings. Next, senior administrators need to do the same. This needs to be followed by faculty leaders, staff leaders, deans, department chairs, etc. It should be an overt, well-articulated statement of how all public forums will operate, and then the standards must be enforced. In addition, some individuals who lack civility may have other unstated issues. This type of behavior can be a manifestation of unresolved hostility toward the organization or individuals within the organization. If appropriate, perhaps that behavior should be investigated so that either the hostility can be resolved (which may solve the civility issue) or to insure the hostility does not escalate.

Changing a culture is not easy, and it can be slow. However, with a good plan, good intentions, support of the board and the chancellor (if appropriate), trust, and consistency in the CEO, it can be done. Make sure you are in for the long haul if you set out on this task. Changing CEOs every two or three years will not result in a lasting change in a college culture.

5

Multi-College District Tensions

VINEYARD SYMPOSIUM ISSUES

- Reducing the feeling among sister colleges that they are treated unfairly. Frequently, these feelings are:

  - budget allocations and budget reductions between colleges;

  - large established college(s) vs. smaller new college(s) (the resource distribution model is seen as unfair by both for opposite reasons);

  - unequal ability by colleges to raise additional revenue outside of the allocation model; and

  - conflict created by the chancellor and/or the board by forcing comparison or competition between colleges or by creating feelings of favoritism.

- Reducing the conflict between the colleges and the district. For example:

  - district believes that colleges have competing interests and they are working from self-interest and not working to benefit the entire district;

  - district protects itself at the expense of the colleges; and

  - district wants to control the colleges as much as possible yet success requires a level of college autonomy.

- Reducing interpersonal conflicts among district CEOs. More specifically, between:

  - presidents;

  - a president and the chancellor; and

  - a president and the board without being protected by the chancellor.

- Relating multi-college tensions to single-college districts with educational centers.

Depending on a person's experience and on the specific situation, a multi-college district can be seen as either a blessing or a curse. Occasionally, it can be both at the same time. The dilemma of a multi-college district is finding a way to capitalize on the benefits of being multiple colleges working together without penalizing colleges for being in a multi-college district. Coinciding with this dilemma is the issue of how a multi-college district should operate in terms of centralization and decentralization of authority. The benefits of a multi-college district are primarily a function of its size. The most commonly recognized benefit is economies of scale which can embrace everything from purchasing to administrative information systems to staffing and external expertise. Of course, to capture the economies of scale, those functions must be centralized. The goal is to identify the areas where the benefits of centralization outweigh the negative impact from the loss of college autonomy. This same analysis needs to be extended to administrative operations (e.g. selected administrative services and human resources) where the cost savings and benefits of being centralized exceed the benefits lost from not having the operations duplicated at each college. If this optimum balance can be achieved, there is a distinct benefit to being in a multi-college district. There is also the centralized benefit of labor negotiations. Only one contract for each labor unit is negotiated at the district level and the colleges do not have to be directly involved. The other major benefit is political. The level of political influence exerted by multi-college districts exceeds what would be possible as single-college districts because of the efforts of operating on a centralized basis. Many people also feel it is an advantage that there is only one board of trustees and the responsibility for interaction with that board is at the district level, not the college level. Without belaboring the point, there are distinct benefits that can be derived from being part of a multi-college district, and the question for a college is at what cost (both in dollars and autonomy) were those benefits achieved.

There are diseconomies of scale as well. Most notable is the amount of time and energy spent in coordination of the different colleges within the district and with the central bureaucracy to accomplish tasks. As the multi-college district grows in size, these challenges also grow proportionately. Furthermore, at some size, the cost of centralized operations exceeds the savings due to the staffing expense incurred in the effort to coordinate the operations at multiple colleges.

When the colleges as a group feel either too much autonomy has been lost or district expenses are too large, it is easier to wrestle with the problem because at least the colleges are unanimous in their objections. This, of course, assumes a willingness by the chancellor and board to alter district operations and relinquish some authority to the colleges. Theoretically, a multi-college district should be able to achieve optimum balance between centralization and decentralization to maximize economies of scale while leaving each college with the maximum level of necessary autonomy. Of course, theory and practice are two different things, and, again, the challenge is greater the larger the district.

Perhaps, in a different venue, a more comprehensive analysis should be conducted to examine the differences between single-college districts and multi-college districts as well as the differences among different sizes of multi-college districts. In the Vineyard Symposium, those differences were not the issue. CEOs accepted the general structure of the multi-college district they inherited with their position as a college president and instead wanted to focus on issues of operating within that structure.

Tensions Between Colleges

It is a harder problem to solve when the tensions exist between colleges because a particular college feels it is treated unfairly. In these situations, there are often only win/lose positions and no win/win options. The most bitter fights between colleges involve the distribution of district resources among the colleges through the district allocation model.

All community colleges in California (maybe in the entire U.S.) are underfunded. It means every community college feels it is not receiving adequate funds to accomplish its core mission. Under these circumstances, whenever an organization has to determine how to allocate a fixed amount of money, the discussion can quickly become emotional and combative. This is true in the state legislature when elected officials determine the amount of funds for community colleges versus other state agencies, in the Board of Governors when members determine the formulas for distribution among districts, and within districts when trustees determine the allocation among colleges – sometimes even between departments within a college. They are all win/lose discussions - the worst kind.

When a multi-college district looks at an allocation model for its colleges, there is a fundamental decision that must be made. Will the model essentially be a pass-through model in which revenues are distributed as they are earned, or will the district allocate the total fixed revenues through a locally designed redistribution system? While there are times a redistribution system is preferred to meet unique, local situations or needs, most districts prefer a pass-through system. Most efforts to design unique allocation systems have usually tried to allocate funds by differentiating on the basis of cost variables (curriculum mix, staffing costs, facility distinctions, etc.). Inevitably, it is realized there are so many cost variables between colleges that, even after many of these distinctions are made, it is still thought to be unfair because some variables have been left out of the formula. Besides, an enormously complex allocation model has been created that few people understand and that often leads to the model being "gamed" by those few who do understand it. Conversely, in the California community colleges, the state has developed a very simple allocation model, primarily using base funding and distribution per FTES. In the case of California, a pass-through model has the advantage of creating an understandable process, and each college feels it is receiving the money it earned. There is no reallocation to the "other college."

A college may not like the result, but it is based on the reality of how the district received funds and as a result, it is at least usually perceived as being fair.

When a district uses a pass-through allocation model, the allocation model should reflect the way the district receives revenue from the State of California. As stated previously, there is no perfect allocation model, and creating different redistribution models within the district will only tend to create beliefs by some that they are not receiving the money they earned. However, a pass-through model means the district is creating the same incentives for the colleges that the state has created for the district. When a district creates its own models, unintended incentives can be created which work against maximizing revenue from the state. Finally, whether a college likes the state model or not, a pass-through model means each college is working with the current reality and, in turn, means the colleges should work together for change at the state level instead of fighting each other.

The allocation model should encourage prudent fiscal management and entrepreneurial efforts by allowing colleges to retain their ending balance and all the dedicated income they have generated.

The allocation model should find a method for holding colleges accountable for meeting their FTES goals. Creating targets and budgeting for those targets is a necessary part of the process, but at some point colleges need to be accountable for meeting or not meeting those goals. Community colleges now live in the era of accountability, and the same should be true for fiscal management. Furthermore, if there is no accountability, an incentive of generating FTES below the goal level could be created so that a college reduces its expenses without reducing its revenues. For this to be effective, a district must develop data-driven enrollment projections for each college that provide the basis for the allocation of funded FTES.

Likewise, if the allocation model is a pass-through of the state allocation model, budget reductions should be treated the same way. The district should reduce college budgets (and funded FTES) in accordance with the manner in which the state has reduced district funds. Again, colleges may not like it, but at least it is viewed as fair.

If a district chooses to provide temporary redistributions within in the allocation model (e.g. a new college or a natural disaster at one of the colleges), it is a good idea to define "temporary" up front. By defining up front when the provision will expire, the district can avoid arguments down the road when there is an attempt to return to normal operations.

The conflicts within districts between the "big" colleges and the "small" colleges is common. The big colleges have an economic advantage because of economies of scale, but the state allocation model adjusts for that by giving a larger base allocation to smaller colleges. That is the beauty of the pass-through allocation model as it is giving each college the revenue it earned and corresponds to the revenue the college would receive if it were a single-college district. If the district is operated properly, each college should also be making a smaller contribution to the district than it would have to pay to duplicate those services as a single-college district.

As a system, colleges need to move away from the idea that bigger is better. If a small college has a documented strategy to grow that is supported by data, the district should try to make it happen because that growth should improve the overall efficiency of the district. Unfortunately, too often it is just wishful thinking by the small college without a clear path to growth. There are many advantages to being smaller and developing strategies for operating efficiently as a smaller college. The goal of the district needs to be to have each college achieve its optimum size for its service area demands and, in turn, develop maximum efficiency for each college at that optimum size. However, there needs to be resistance to the thirst to just be bigger and to fund efforts of increasing college size that are not based on sound strategies and data.

When it comes to the differences between colleges to raise money outside the allocation model, it must be recognized that no two colleges are ever equal. Likewise, no two colleges are alike in terms of enrollment demand, student preparation, competition, community support, etc. It is even true in terms of college leadership. Raising money outside the allocation model is just one other area. A district cannot equalize all differences. At some point, after resolving issues within the allocation model, the district needs to let colleges go and encourage them to exploit their strengths and reap the benefits of their ingenuity and entrepreneurial spirit. Otherwise, the incentives will be killed, and colleges that are dependent on the district will be created.

Sometimes a multi-college district can become dysfunctional because of inappropriate comparisons and competition between colleges. This in turn also usually leads to feelings of favoritism towards one of the colleges. There is only one person who can fix this problem – the chancellor. If the chancellor is the source of the problem, the presidents need to speak to him or her as a group. The chancellor may be unaware of the harm being created. If the board of trustees is the problem, the presidents need to help the chancellor understand that he or she has the responsibility to fix it because if the presidents try to fix it, the chancellor's authority will be undermined. The board may not be able to see the harm being inflicted so the chancellor will need to suggest alternative ways for the board to accomplish the same goal. All forms of public college accountability will create comparisons (and perhaps competition) without any additional pressure or comparisons from the board. Any necessary comparisons can occur through president evaluations. Inevitably, all presidents always watch accountability measures, and the presidents are making the relevant comparisons. Besides, usually the newspapers will make the comparisons without the board needing to do it.

Since the state Chancellor's Office provides the public uniform data on student performance for every college, each college needs to be prepared to respond to its unfavorable data and how the college plans to improve in those areas. Furthermore, since comparisons between colleges within a district are inevitable, what the presidents, chancellor, and board need to do is figure out how to make the comparisons meaningful and fair. The district should establish its own report with the necessary qualifications of the data. The report should define the appropriate basis for comparisons up front (preferably before the data are released) and not let external agencies impose the criteria on the district. Colleges within the district cannot avoid comparisons, but they can control how the comparisons are made and the manner in which the comparisons are delivered. Incidentally, the relevant comparisons for some of the colleges may be with colleges outside the district and not with the sister colleges within the district. In the end, the district needs to develop a way for this to be a positive experience (emphasize the positive outcomes, describe the plans for how the college will use data to help fix problems, etc.) as opposed to just denigrating colleges with poor performance outcomes.

Financial performance is the other arena in which comparisons between colleges are frequently made by the board of trustees. Again, the board needs to understand that "brow beating" a college president or constantly mentioning the issues facing a college in public session doesn't help. All presidents want their college to be financially successful. The goal has to be for the district and the sister colleges to develop a process that makes all colleges within the district financially successful.

The comparability is even more notable when a college establishes an educational center. There are usually two types of educational centers. One type is a center that is focused on a small number of instructional disciplines, and there is no intent of the center ever becoming an independent college. The other type is where the center is being developed and grown with the intent of one day being an independently accredited institution. In the latter case, it is only a matter of time until the single-college district becomes a multi-college district. In those cases, the district should think about the potential tensions from the outset because it is easier to manage a planned evolution than it is to suddenly have to change the method of operation when the center reaches a critical size. All colleges need to find their optimum place on the centralization-decentralization continuum, and educational centers just add to that necessity.

Conflict between a College and the District

Ideally, the goals of the district coincide (or at least are not in conflict) with the goals of the college. Likewise, ideally, the delineation of functions between the colleges and the district have been agreed upon so that economies of scale and college autonomy are maximized (or at least agreed upon by all parties). However, there is always the possibility of tension because the district is focused on the whole, and the college is focused on its part. Communities, students, faculty, etc. tend to think in terms of colleges while boards of trustees, district offices, and chancellors tend to think in terms of the total district. The larger the district, the greater the likelihood that this tension will exist. When it does, separate the areas so it is clear where the interests of the college and the district coincide and where they do not. Focus on where the interests do not coincide and work to find a solution – usually it is related to funding or the freedom to do something different from the other colleges. The most successful solutions occur when the district philosophy is that the district will prosper as student success is increased. When that solution is not possible, the nature of the responsibility and authority of the chancellor and the board is that they must protect what is in the best interest of the district. As difficult as it may be, the board and chancellor must get people to think about the good of the whole and the fact that the college and the district operate with one bottom line in mind: student success. Keeping the team focused in that way can sometimes ease the tensions. In most multi-college districts, the service areas are very different and have different populations requiring different solutions. Try to keep everyone's focus on being educators first and recognizing that it is not one size fits all. Every effort should be made to avoid these situations, but college presidents must understand that it is the price that must be paid for being part of a larger system. It is the same type of price that is paid by all community colleges for being part of a state system. The state makes decisions that are in the best interest of the state system, even though at times they are not in the best interest of an individual college.

Interpersonal Conflicts

When interpersonal conflicts arise involving a college president, all solutions must work through the chancellor. It is his or her responsibility to solve conflicts between presidents as well as between a president and a board member. Presidents experiencing these conflicts must meet face to face with the chancellor and seek his or her help. When the conflict is between the chancellor and a president, it is best resolved through direct communication. If unsuccessful, the president must wait for the chancellor to leave, or the president must either leave or live with the conflict. The president should not go around the chancellor to the board and should not engage the faculty to fight on the president's behalf. If the president takes either of these actions, it will create a show-down with the chancellor in a win/lose conflict. The president might prevail but at a cost. The chancellor may lose the battle but continue to serve as chancellor over a rebellious president. The chancellor may still have the backing of the board and will prevail in future conflicts. At best, unless the chancellor leaves, a very difficult working relationship has been created. If the president does not prevail, it not only creates a difficult working relationship with the chancellor, but it will also hurt the president when applying for other jobs. The possibility of these conflicts should serve as a reminder that when seeking a job as a president in a multi-college district, interview the chancellor. It can be either the best or worst presidency depending on one's relationship with the chancellor. The applicant should also determine the relationship between the chancellor and the board. Conflict between the board and the chancellor can impair a president's ability to lead a college, and, worse yet, the president can become embroiled in the conflict.

At the same time, college presidents must recognize they have a much narrower perspective of the district as a whole than the chancellor because of their focus on an individual college. Colleges and districts are hierarchical organizations. Accordingly, the position of the chancellor must be respected even if the president does not "like" the chancellor. The chancellor is CEO of the whole district organization. As a result, the chancellor reports to and is the board's representative and supervises the college president.

The issues and tensions of a multi-college district are mostly issues related to funding and centralization versus decentralization of authority. Problems and challenges are magnified by the size of the operation with larger districts having even more struggles than smaller multi-college districts. However, it is possible to have similar tensions within an individual college. All organizations should try to determine the lowest level possible in the organization for decision making while maintaining a necessary level of organizational control and economy of scale. A CEO in a single-college district could look at everything discussed in this chapter and see possible applicability within a single college because every organization continually wrestles with the centralization-decentralization question.

6

Board Of Trustees

- Insuring the board will stay supportive of the CEO in the face of employee criticism when the CEO is simply implementing a board directive.

- Helping CEOs provide more communication with their trustees when they are consumed with issues on campus or in the community.

- Helping CEOs avoid being preoccupied with being "one election away from losing their job."

The dilemma posed by a board of trustees within the community college system is that there is such disparity among the different boards within the system. It is even more confusing because there are frequently enormous differences between individual board members who are sitting on the same board of trustees. Those management challenges are exacerbated by the fact that, due to the election cycle, the composition can change every two years and that a chancellor or a president serves at the discretion of each new board. Therefore, a chancellor or president is effectively reporting to five or seven "bosses" who are all different and don't speak with a single voice! This, of course, violates a fundamental tenet of management which suggests that reporting, accountability, and responsibility for delegation of authority should connect to a single person (or at least a single voice). If that isn't stressful enough, because of the Brown Act, the chancellor or president must conduct virtually all the district's or college's business with the board in a public setting with public comments.

Because trustees are publicly elected, there are inevitable differences between and within boards regarding experience as a board member. For many, it is the first, elected office they have held. It is this lack of experience or disparity in experience that leads to the most common issue between a board of trustees and the CEO – how to help boards understand their proper role and avoid acting in an improper manner. The difficulty is that CEOs are being placed in the role of teaching their "boss" how to do the job. There is the added problem that most, new CEOs have never been board members and, in many cases, their previous position only had limited interaction with the board of trustees. For all these reasons, on-going training for the board of trustees is a must. It is definitely easier to have board training done by a third party whom the board respects. The key is to find the right person for each particular board. Is it a board member from a college that is respected? Is it an officer from the statewide trustee organization? Is it a politician? Is it someone from the business community? The difficulty is finding the person whose advice and counsel board members will take seriously. Of course, this assumes each board member has an open mind to receiving advice. Once that has happened, the CEO can keep referring to the advice. It might also be helpful to have a separate session for the board chair and vice chair because they have a critical role in keeping the board under control and providing the necessary board leadership to create a well-operating board of trustees. Again, after the training session, the CEO can keep referring to the advice in helping these two people perform their job. It needs to be clear the board chair and vice chair are not just honorary board positions; they need to model appropriate behavior and, ideally, that behavior would then be replicated by the other board members.

Even if an outside trainer is used to develop and strengthen board skills, CEOs need to make the independent effort to develop their own knowledge about how trustees can operate properly and become a policy board. An outline has been provided in Appendix A which provides guidelines for the role of a board chair. In most cases, these same principles can be applied to all members of the board of trustees. Also, a commonly referenced book on the subject is *Boards That Make a Difference* by John Carver. These are just two possible references for expanding knowledge on proper board behavior and performance. The critical point is for CEOs to recognize that the partnership and relationship between them and the board is so critical that CEOs should not just try to learn as they go. CEOs should sit through all training with the board of trustees because it is a partnership, and the CEOs need to learn about proper board behavior and to be sure they are doing everything possible to make the board successful. Just don't stop there. Besides the training, work to build an independent knowledge base and a collection of best practices from other, more experienced CEOs.

Legal Requirements
Through the help of a general counsel or outside attorney, the CEO should be completely familiar with the Brown Act and the limits of public record requests. With this legal expertise, the CEO should arrange for both these areas to be included in a separate board training session (along with at least a general understanding of other legal limits – unfair labor practices, discriminatory hiring practices, awarding processes for public contracts, etc.). The easiest way to avoid lawsuits and public actions against the board is to educate the board so that missteps don't ever happen in the first place.

Board Member Behavior
When the board of trustees conduct as a whole is operating properly, but an individual board member is not behaving properly, the board must take responsibility for managing the behavior of that individual board member. The corrective action probably needs to come from the board chair, with the support of the other board members. It should not be delegated to the CEO. It may be possible for the CEO to find someone to help the board chair think out

a solution and how to interact with the board member in question, but it should be done without the direct involvement of the CEO. When the CEO is involved, there may be residual hard feelings and the board member in question may feel the chair and CEO are "ganging up on him." The board member may also feel it is not the CEO's place to tell him or her how to perform as a board member. The corrective effort is not to make this interaction disciplinary in nature but rather to help a board member understand the proper role. However, there are certain types of behavior that cannot be tolerated, and it is the board chair's responsibility to make all board members understand the limits on individual choices of behavior and to enforce those limits.

Just as noted in the aforementioned situation, friction between board members also needs to be resolved by the board chair. Again, this type of facilitation may not be part of the board chair's skill set, so an outside person may need to be brought in, but the CEO should not be the facilitator.

In the case of friction between board members and faculty leaders, the CEO must be involved. Any time the board interacts with anyone inside the college, the CEO must be involved. CEOs never want to condone interactions around them – even in conflict resolution. Again, it may be appropriate to involve an outsider, but the CEO must be a direct participant in the resolution.

Expectations and Directives
If the board of trustees and the CEO are going to have a true working partnership and a solid relationship, they need to take time to develop clearly stated, mutual expectations. In so doing, all parties need to try to be as honest and as specific as possible. So many problems can be avoided by having everyone's expectations stated and understood by all parties.

An example of where this is helpful is when the board has requested that the CEO make a controversial decision or directive.

To start, there needs to be a frank dialogue between the CEO and the board about the merits and consequences of such an action. Hopefully, everyone agrees it is the right thing to do, the right way to do it, and everyone is proceeding "with their eyes wide open." Before proceeding, the topic of mutual expectations should be revisited and understood with a reaffirmation of the board's continued support in the face of the expected employee criticism. The even more difficult situation is when the board is directing the CEO to do something the CEO thinks is wrong. Of course, there are two types of disagreement – strategic as opposed to immoral or illegal. In the case of strategic disagreement, it is best to avoid conflict before it ever arrives at the point of action and instead explore alternative ways to achieve the same goal at the outset of the discussion. The CEO should not let the dialogue arrive at the point where he or she is between "a rock and a hard place" with the board and the CEO in a win/lose decision. Usually CEOs can convince the board that it is the board's role to define the goal or policy and the CEO's role to define the strategy to achieve it, particularly if that is clarified at the outset of the discussion. If situations have really deteriorated, it is probably time to go back to a frank discussion of the roles of a policy board and the roles of the CEO. The CEO cannot allow a specific situation to set a precedent and dictate a change in the future roles of both the board and the CEO.

If the disagreement is over the goal or policy, work to modify the goal so all parties can support it. Boards usually see the political benefit in having a unified effort and, accordingly, see the importance of having an outcome the CEO can support. In trying to bring about the modification, it is a lot easier at the beginning of the discussion than it is at the end. It may also be necessary to dissect the request to understand the true motivation of the policy request as well as a full understanding of the CEO's objection. Using those components, try to develop a mutually acceptable policy. However, CEOs must always be prepared to refuse to do something they feel would be harmful or detrimental to the college. Preserving the job is not more important than one's personal integrity. If the CEO has worked to build a partnership relationship with the board, it is rare this refusal is necessary.

In the case of immoral or illegal directives, don't acquiesce. If the board cannot be dissuaded from making this entirely inappropriate directive, be sure to include a discussion of the item in a public session of the board meeting, along with your response included in the minutes. Place the item on the board agenda as a discussion item or ask for direction on it in the CEO report given in open session. If neither of those approaches works, put objections in writing and send them individually to each board member in a formal letter so that your position is documented if issues arise.

Communication

A more common problem resulting from inadequately expressed expectations is communication between the CEO and the board of trustees. In particular, there needs to be an explicit discussion as to what communication the board expects on a regular basis and on an emergency basis. Failing to meet board expectations on communication can be one of the biggest problems for the CEO, and it is usually a result of the CEO not having a clear understanding of what the board wants. Whatever is agreed to must be a top priority for the CEO. A bigger issue is when different board members want different amounts and types of communication. As a general rule, all board members should be provided with the same information and in the same time frame. Some board members want a lot of attention and others only want to work on a "need to know" basis. If different board members are going to be treated differently, it must be with the consent and understanding of the full board. Be careful of this differential treatment. For example, board members who want more attention may say they don't want to be treated differently, but they want to have breakfast with you every week. Situations like this result in differential treatment and should be avoided or done consistently with all board members or done differentially with the consent of the board.

Usually, the communication with the board chair and vice chair are different and more frequent, but the whole board should know what is happening. The question of whether to include the vice chair in these meetings varies among CEOs. The logic is that the vice chair is often being groomed to be a chair and by including him/her ahead of time, a smoother transition can take place. The inclusion also helps to validate expectations of the access provided to the board chair. The other benefit is that two people, not just one, are prepared to deal with board meetings and other college business. The presence of both board members also eliminates any questions about what was or was not discussed in the meetings with the CEO.

Successful communication between the CEO and board members is one of the critical elements in having a successful relationship and partnership between the board and the CEO. Explicitly define the communication that will be provided by the CEO. Look for easy ways to meet the board's needs (e.g. weekly emails on the state of the college, verbal reports in board meetings), but give them what they need. When communicating in writing to the board, be mindful of public records requests and the Brown Act requirements. Written communication to the board can be a resource in demonstrating and solidifying the appropriate role of both the CEO, individual board members, and the board as a whole.

Working with a board of trustees requires considerable time and patience and offers a variety of growth opportunities for the CEO. Because boards in California are elected by the public and represent community members, many of whom attended community colleges, board members bring an interesting perspective and a variety of experiences that can contribute greatly to the success of students. Providing training in effective boardsmanship, building a relationship/partnership with the board individually and collectively, and ensuring board members understand the mission of community colleges are the CEOs primary duties in this area. Doing so will ensure trustees fulfill their fiduciary responsibilities in an appropriate manner.

7

Participatory Governance

- Redefining faculty involvement and roles in governance when they have become blurred with collective bargaining (especially when efforts of definition are taken as a discussion of personality, not process).

- Improving governance processes when some faculty question every decision and continually want to return to a past practice of faculty control as opposed to participative governance.

The process of participatory governance can be very frustrating for CEOs, but when it is done properly by all parties, the process actually improves the operation and decision making of the college. Participatory governance is a simple by-product of the management style of leadership known as participatory management. Douglas McGregor, through his book *The Human Side of Enterprise* (1960), described his Theory Y which provided the tenets for participatory management. Subsequent work amplified on his principles and in particular found that participatory management was especially effective in certain work environments. One of those environments was in settings like higher education. While many California community colleges practiced participatory management in the 1970s and early 1980s, not all colleges did. As a result, in 1988, AB 1725 was passed by the legislature which placed a mandate on colleges to practice elements of participatory management, particularly with the faculty. As a result of this legislation, Title 5 regulations were developed which outline the minimum requirements for participatory governance between the district board and its faculty, staff, and students. The fundamental mandate within Title 5 regulations is that the governing board adopt policies for academic senate participation in district and college governance – providing, at a minimum, the governing board or its designees would consult collegially with the academic senate when adopting policies and procedures on academic and professional matters. "Consult collegially" was defined in terms of relying primarily on the advice and judgment of the academic senate or through a defined process to reach mutual agreement. Furthermore, the "academic and professional matters" were defined by the well-known list of ten plus one. Everyone should read the actual Title 5 passage (Section 53200) because one of the first sources of problems is a common misunderstanding of what the regulations say and require of the board of trustees or its designee. Actual practices vary among districts because the regulations are minimums and the governing board can adopt policies or practices beyond the minimums.

These current writings are not the place to dissect the actual code language since there are now many sources of information that can provide that analysis. However, the problems related to the enforcement of these regulations are a frequent topic at the Vineyard Symposium. As mentioned above, too many people have never read the regulation. The coining of the term "shared governance" and its frequent use demonstrates a misinterpretation of Title 5, Section 53200. Shared governance is not a term used in any of the Title 5 language. A good starting point for a college is to have administrators and faculty leaders jointly read Section 53200 and agree on its meaning. Once the regulations are reviewed, it is apparent that participative management is not a delegation of authority, but rather it is an assurance faculty will provide input to the board of trustees (or its designee) on policies and procedures (through a manner described in Section 53200) on academic and professional matters as defined in Section 53200. This defined form of participative management in California community colleges is what is meant by participative governance.

It would also help college leaders to understand the intent of the regulation by also understanding the underlying management theory of participative management, starting with McGregor's Theory Y and all subsequent refinement of that theory. In 1988, there were still numerous examples within California of very authoritarian management practices. AB 1725 was trying to move the system to a more enlightened form of management and to reduce the disparity among colleges when it came to faculty involvement. However, it was never the intent to delegate the board's authority to the academic senate, nor to create a town hall form of decision making. Many of the problems that have resulted from these Title 5 regulations would be resolved if all parties understood the actual language of the regulation and the original intent of the legislation.

Participatory governance has a fundamental element of working on a representative basis. When those representatives don't reflect the thoughts and beliefs of their constituency, it is a problem for the administration. Title 5 seems to clearly state the academic senate is the representative body of the faculty for participatory governance. When leaders of the academic senate don't adequately represent the faculty (and the faculty are not willing to replace them), it is difficult to find a way around them. First, when faculty complain about the leaders, it is important to explain to them that electing appropriate leaders is their responsibility, and it is not possible for the administration to become involved in making changes in that leadership. However, it is sometimes useful for the CEO to encourage strong, potential candidates to become involved. Second, there are sometimes strong elements within the academic senate who can provide important input to decisions. For example, in colleges with elected department chairs, those chairs often operate as a committee within the academic senate. For many academic and professional matters, this is actually a more relevant source of input than the entire academic senate and, as such, is maintaining the spirit of Title 5. It is also easily explained as to why it is the chosen route for participation as opposed to involving the entire senate. If those chairs also engage their departments, there are usually fewer complaints about lack of faculty involvement in decision making because department chairs can more readily provide a good communication system with the entire faculty.

Another area that can also create problems in this representative structure is that sometimes the academic senate does not realize the limits of the authorization to be involved in the decision-making process in Title 5. Again, that is why it is important to review the definition of "consult collegially" and the definition of "academic and professional matters." CEOs can always extend either of these definitions, but they are in essence relinquishing management rights, and they are setting a precedent that extends the authorization of Title 5. Once extended, it is often hard to reverse in the future. If the Title 5 authorization is going to be extended, it should be done on the basis of an individual situation and not by formally adding new categories to the Title 5 definition.

When the problem is a lack of communication between the academic senate and the faculty at large, there is a role for the administration to play in helping to remedy the problem. Since the communication involves information about how faculty are involved in the decision-making process as well as the substance of that involvement, it helps the CEO when faculty are informed. Often complaints arise from faculty simply because they were not informed as to what was happening. Working with the senate to distribute information helps everyone. While CEOs can argue it is not their problem, dissent from lack of perceived involvement can become the CEO's problem when the CEO acts on the academic senate recommendation. It is better to fix the communication problem so CEOs know the full spectrum of response before acting, or they could be blind-sided by unstated, yet significant, opposition. Furthermore, if the faculty are informed and don't like the actions of the academic senate, the leaders will be held accountable by their constituents and necessary change will be initiated by the faculty at large. CEOs are helped by having a fully informed faculty, including providing information about the faculty's own organization, the academic senate.

Vision

Beyond the interaction with the academic senate on the areas delineated in Title 5, there are also other areas in which participatory governance is appropriate, even though it is not mandated. One of those areas is the development of a vision for the college. CEOs usually have their own ideas about what needs to be contained in the vision for the college, but to be effective, the vision for the college needs to be embraced by the college community. There cannot be competing visions, so, at some level, all ideas must be merged into a single vision or at least prioritized. Ideally, a vision is collaboratively developed under the leadership of the CEO. The development of the vision needs to start with everyone agreeing on the relevant data. If everyone doesn't start at the same place, they won't end up at the same place. The data are important because it is one of the critical elements in forming an authentic vision. The collected data is the current appraisal of the college, the environment outside the college, and the forecast for the community and the state. Once there is agreement on the data, the next step is to gain agreement on what the college should look like in five years (or some other agreed-upon time frame). If everyone can agree on where to start and where to end, it is easier to agree on how to achieve the vision. People will help implement a vision that makes sense to them. They need to understand the purpose and the reasoning for the vision which includes an understanding of how the data identified critical elements within the vision. The college community will also work harder to accomplish the vision if they helped to develop it. CEOs cannot let the vision development process disintegrate into competing visions, but instead do what is necessary for the college to build the vision collaboratively.

A college vision is not a slogan; it is a concept of the future with at least five critical elements:

1. how to make the organization distinctive and uniquely better;
2. how to solve the organization's problems;
3. how to generate sufficient revenue and control expenses (live within budget) to accomplish the vision;
4. how to increase student success; and
5. how to build off the strategic advantages of the college.

A vision is not something that can be imposed by power or authority because the people within the college have to believe in that vision and want to make it happen. At the same time, the vision should contain elements that invoke the passion of the CEO so that the necessary energy can be supplied to make it a reality. If it lacks collaborative support or the passion of the CEO, the vision will sit on the shelf.

At the same time the CEO is collaboratively building a vision with the college community, the CEO must also be engaging the board of trustees. This is a delicate situation. There must be enough prior discussion with the board to be sure the vision will be developed within the board's broad priorities while at the same time assuring the college community their involvement is meaningful. As discussed previously, this involvement of the board needs to be consistent with the concept of being a policy board and having the board trust the development of the vision under the leadership of the CEO. In the end, the development of a meaningful vision is a real challenge to the leadership skills of the CEO.

Faculty Unions
Within the faculty at many colleges, there are often individual faculty who serve in a leadership capacity in both the academic

senate and the faculty union. This common leadership can lead to a blurred distinction between the role of the academic senate and the role of the faculty union. Since there are separate regulations regarding the faculty union's rights, it is useful for a college to develop a delineation of function between the academic senate and the faculty union so that all parties, including the administration, know how to appropriately interact with the representatives of the faculty. Some faculty groups will resist doing this because they may feel there is more power to both groups by having ill-defined roles. However, with a lack of delineation, topics may be discussed in both arenas. Besides creating confusion (particularly if the outcomes are different), there is an excess expenditure of institutional time and energy for something that should have only been discussed once. If there is resistance to creating a delineation of function, the reasoning for it needs to be described as a necessary procedural activity that will transcend any specific leader (senate or union or college president). Furthermore, delineation of function agreements is an important part of the accreditation process for describing institutional participation. More importantly, it is helpful to administrators and board members to be sure appropriate processes are followed and new employees understand how the college works and how recommendations are formed. A college always benefits from clearing up ambiguity about decision making. In particular, the process for receiving input and recommendations as well as designating where the delegated authority rests for making different decisions should be clarified. A clearly defined decision-making process also improves accountability for actions or lack of actions throughout the process.

Past Practices

One of the real dilemmas for a new CEO is inheriting past practices the CEO perceives to be ill-advised or inappropriate, yet embraced by the faculty. The most common example of this dilemma is in the area of participatory governance where either the academic senate has been delegated authority beyond Title 5 and/or the union has managed to negotiate away management rights. Changing the past practice has to start by clarifying the roles and trying to make them consistent with Title 5 and the Education Code. That can be difficult because the faculty groups are probably happy with the past practice and see no need to change. Gaining clarification of roles may require a third party representing faculty interests. Perhaps a current or former state academic senate president and union president could be brought in to meet with faculty leaders to clarify the appropriate roles for faculty involvement. Of course, even if the people from outside clarify the legal requirements for involvement, faculty leaders can always say those are minimums and that the administration and the board can delegate more authority (in some cases previous administrations did just that, both in union contracts and senate involvement). The best way to back out of that is to have the board of trustees talk about accountability. Whoever is being held accountable needs to have the authority to make the decision and be removed for poor decisions. There is no way for the board or the CEO to remove senate or union leaders or committees (or in some cases department chairs) so the authority must rest elsewhere. If those changes are made, the board or the CEO needs to follow through on accountability so that the issue of accountability is demonstrated to be real. The bigger problem is when authority has been given away in union contracts. That requires a change in the next contract and will require some concessions in other areas. Once the slate has been swept clean, it would be useful for the college to write a delineation of function as described previously and a description of the decision-making process so representation can be removed from oral history and tradition.

While many CEOs have horror stories about misguided participatory governance, if the participation is properly defined and legitimately implemented by all sides, it is a superior form of decision making. Genuine, participative decision making in a college setting takes advantage of gaining input from valuable human resources within the institution and creates decisions that are more readily embraced by the college community because people feel they were part of the process. It is worth the effort of the CEO to make it right and make it work. A college with a dynamic form of participation is an energetic institution on the path to excellence.

8

Dealing With Diversity In The Community

VINEYARD SYMPOSIUM ISSUES

- Interacting with advocacy groups (internal as well as external) that are trying to inappropriately influence decisions. Examples of the type of decisions are personnel decisions, educational programs, and geographic preferences.

- Handling advocacy that appears to be racially or ethnically based.

- Dealing with advocacy groups when they start to make hostile, public attacks and unprofessional comments.

- Handling public controversy when it is caused by comments from an employee.

- Deciding how a college should reflect its community.

- Working with blanket public record requests from newspapers or community groups.

- Coping with the feeling of always being on the "hot seat" because the media is waiting to pounce.

- Living with the stress created by serving a struggling community and not having adequate resources to meet the educational needs of the community.

A "community" college receives that label because there is a greater connection between the local college and the local community than there is among any other form of higher education and surrounding community. This connection between the community college and its community results in the CEO experiencing diversity in a variety of forms, including ethnic, racial, and cultural issues and political views.

In California, the community college system is geographically organized by districts which defines the political entity that supports each college (single college districts) or colleges (multi-college districts). The community within those district boundaries is responsible for electing the district board of trustees, passing and paying for bond issues, and committing a portion of their property taxes to fund the colleges. Beyond the legal relationship between the community and the colleges, local communities are involved in almost every imaginable form – from advisory committees to serving on CEO searches, from participation at board meetings to supporting cultural activities at the college, and, of course, the college's students and employees usually live in the local community.

Communities take great pride in their local community college. That pride and enthusiasm infuse vitality into a college. However, with that connection, a community can feel it has a personal relationship with a college and can have high expectations regarding the level of influence and involvement it should have within the college. That sense of ownership can create a tension between the community and the college administration and/or the board of trustees. First, because the college is a source of community pride, any matters related to the college will often engage locally elected officials beyond the board of trustees. When there are disagreements, this can add more parties and more opinions to the disagreement. Second, when there is a sense of ownership, community members may feel they need to be consulted on all major matters at the college. On some issues (facilities, land acquisition, etc.) this is not a problem because community consultation would be a normal part of the college process. However, there are other issues that are felt to be the domain of the institution (curriculum changes, personnel decisions, etc.), and conflict can occur when the community feels they were not adequately involved in the final decision. Third, the feeling of ownership can create a problem with regard to the use of college facilities for community activities (youth sports, community meetings, community cultural events, etc.). In some cases, the problem is access; and, in other cases, it is the cost to the community group for the use of the facilities. Fourth, in cases where a lack of resources inhibits the ability of the CEO to bring change quickly enough in struggling communities, pressure can be applied by the community, resulting in stressful situations. In all cases, the goal is to ensure the community is involved in the college through the variety of opportunities available to them. The involvement and caring by the community will make the college better. Planned community involvement also helps the community understand how the college operates and how the community's expertise is needed and utilized while at the same time helping the community to learn the appropriate limits for direct community involvement.

A college must know and understand its community, and the community must know and understand the mission and values of the community college. That mutual understanding is important in order for the community college to fulfill its mission in transforming the lives of students. The college has to present itself in a manner that will be welcoming to the community – in a way that will draw members of the community to the college as its first choice for higher education. The college should reflect its community by reflecting the historical aspects of the community where possible, employing community members to work in a variety of areas, and by reflecting the diversity found in the community. In the case of fairly homogenous communities, the college should aim for diversity in an effort to expose the student body and employees to a variety of cultural and ethnic backgrounds.

All CEOs struggle with the frustration of not having adequate resources to fully meet the higher educational needs of the communities served by their colleges. However, that frustration is exacerbated when the CEO serves an underserved community or student population. Being CEO of a college in an underserved community or student population made up of underrepresented students requires a CEO who is committed to service in such a community. The CEO must understand the particular challenges of such a community as well as the related issues for the college in underserved communities. Leading a college in a struggling community can be challenging but also brings significant rewards. Several steps can be undertaken when leading such institutions. The CEO must:

- demonstrate commitment to working in the community;
- promote and/or establish programs and services that support success for the student population;
- create an environment that promotes innovation and creativity for the success of the student population;
- keep the community informed about any success experienced by students and employees in achievement of students' goals; and

- build a culture that celebrates the strengths of students and does not focus on their weaknesses or deficits.

A major challenge for many CEOs occurs when community advocates involve themselves in decisions that are perceived by the CEO to be outside the limits of direct community involvement. In these situations, the tool a CEO must use most is communication. CEOs have to be mindful at all times of their verbal and non-verbal communication and the fact that they are always under the microscope. Every decision they make can be scrutinized. CEOs have the most information on most decisions, and others are looking from the outside and drawing conclusions on limited information. With limited information, those outside the decision-making process "fill in the blanks." The CEO needs to be open and honest in communicating information to any individual or group, keeping in mind the points that are confidential and consistently letting people know the limits of information that can be shared on a particular topic. CEOs need to try to respond to all queries and, within reason, listen to a variety of voices on any number of topics. Not doing so can cause additional problems. Mechanisms should be in place to allow for individuals to give voice to their concerns, allowing them to express opinions in a non-confrontational manner. It will also help CEOs to remember the only behavior they can control is their own.

It can also be helpful to work with the leadership of the advocacy groups on an individual basis, if possible. Members of an advocacy group start positioning behavior and role playing when there are more people present. Try to have the leaders define their desired goals and look for common ground within those goals. Help the advocacy group leaders understand the means for achieving these shared goals is in the purview of the CEO and the board. There is usually far less resistance to agreeing on goals but significant resistance to community efforts to direct the means for achieving the goal. Also, if CEOs are struggling to gain mutual understanding with a community advocacy group leader, they should try using a third party who is trusted by the advocacy group leader.

When there is the added problem of a lack of civility by the community group, again, meet with the group leaders individually. Explain to the leaders how the lack of civil behavior will antagonize people within the college community and make it more difficult to achieve the group's goals. Sometimes, in these situations, a CEO is trying to work with a group leader in which conflict with the college is the goal, not some other more useful purpose. The reason for that motivation is that some leaders maintain their leadership position based on conflict. If the conflict goes away, the group will choose a different leader. The only way to solve this leadership style is to find some goal the college shares with the group's membership so the group wants to work with the college, even if the group's leader objects.

Racially- or ethnically-based controversies can be the most challenging. Despite the challenging nature of such issues, the CEO must take the leadership role and find the heart of the matter without creating further complications. In such situations, CEOs should show interest, objectivity, and fairness to ensure they cannot be accused of insensitivity. In some cases, CEOs must remove themselves and call for an investigation of the issues by someone outside the institution.

"Identity" is at the forefront of what CEOs face. People, especially the disenfranchised, have a deep desire and need for not only representation but inclusion and belonging at every level of the institution. People want to be seen and heard, and the CEO has to be willing to listen and even be uncomfortable with what is being said or the topics or even the people speaking. Advocacy and protest are a huge part of the fabric of educational institutions – from the struggle for the Lesbian, Gay, Bisexual, Transgender (LGBT) studies to anti-apartheid to free speech movements. The voices of students and the actions by colleges and universities have, and continue to have, a huge impact on the fabric of our communities. First, recognizing this rich historical history of advocacy but also recognizing the ways race has played a role in the way social structures are organized and opportunities are given is important. Inherent racism has plagued our nation, and the racial hierarchy people have experienced influences individual behavior of students and employees in our institutions as well as community members. Finding space to listen, but then also finding constructive ways to collaborate to find solutions or make a commitment to an ongoing joint-learning and exploration, is vital. Issues that surface as gender- or LGBT- or racially- or ethnically-based are often intertwined with other issues that also need to be addressed and have exacerbated the feeling that it can be more narrowly defined. Having the opportunity to talk individually helps everyone figure out the actual concerns, puts a human face on the conversation, and helps dispel misconceptions.

CEOs should not use the reasoning that they do not demonstrate overt prejudice. CEOs must recognize the impact of unconscious bias in their own work and the membership of their team. Some recommendations follow for all leaders regardless of ethnicity or race or gender. CEOs need to, at a minimum, commit to the following.

- Recognize and accept they have bias.
- Develop the capacity to check themselves and their decision making to see if there are blind spots or reminders of someone that is triggering reactions and possibly impacting decisions around race, ethnicity, gender, and culture.
- Explore their own awkwardness and discomfort.
- Engage with people they consider different from themselves, and expose themselves to positive role models in that group. If CEOs have concerns about the community

they serve, discern the concerns and find ways to actively engage those people, groups, and issues proactively versus reactively.

- Get feedback and support. Ask for help, admitting what they don't know, and engaging college champions, leaders, and community people who do have passion, expertise, and/or credibility around issues of race and diversity. Most people want to be part of the solution and want things to be better.
- Institutionalize collegewide activities that give people a sense of inclusion and belonging and show they care about them.

Employee-Initiated Controversy
Public comments by employees can cause conflict because of controversial comments that could range from ethnic and race-based issues to cultural issues to political issues to environmental concerns. When comments from an employee cause the controversy, the CEO must proceed carefully. Talk to the employee along with his or her representative to ascertain accurate information about what was said and the circumstances surrounding the statements. The employee may have both first amendment and academic freedom protections, so the CEO needs to proceed with caution if discipline is being considered. It may also be necessary to explain these employee protections to the community who may not understand the actions or lack of discipline by the CEO.

Public Records Requests
Community colleges are public entities and as such they receive more scrutiny than other organizations. That is particularly true in terms of media attention and public records requests. Although receiving a public records request can sometimes make a CEO nervous, it is an obligation that must be fulfilled regardless of the

amount of information requested by an individual. The California Public Records Act, CPRA, requires full cooperation with such requests by members of the public, including the media. Basically, this means a full disclosure of policies and openness in matters of public record except where such information is exempt from disclosure under the CPRA. In order to be prepared for such requests, it is important to have a very clear policy and procedures in place governing the release of information and one point person within the organization to ensure that requests are responded to in a timely manner. The policies and procedures should have been developed with legal assistance, and the point person should be aware of the intricacies of the law regarding such requests and known by individuals within the college or district.

Media Requests
As challenging as dealing with a public records request can be, dealing with the media can be equally challenging. The CEO must develop a level of comfort in doing so and, if necessary, should pursue some professional training. The college also needs to establish a protocol for trustees and managers to follow when dealing with the media which will also create an added level of comfort and reduce the possibility of inconsistencies. The protocol should identify a college spokesperson who responds on behalf of the organization, again to create consistency in the sharing of information. It is a good idea to employ a professional to train managers and trustees in dealing with the media. As a final caution, CEOs should always assume that what they write and what they say will end up in the newspaper or some other public media or as part of a public records request.

Community engagement and involvement in a community college can be one of the great joys of being a community college CEO. It is important to remember a community college has the responsibility to meet the diverse needs of the external community by furthering cultural and economic development. In all communities, but particularly in underserved communities, the college can serve as a respite, offering programs that educate, entertain, and otherwise develop and enhance the lives of community members who are not enrolled in the college. The CEO should ensure the college provides hope inside and outside the college. Hope sustains the pressures and challenges faced daily. It gives one an eye toward the future. Mahatma Gandhi stated, "What is true of the individual will be true of the whole nation if individuals will but refuse to lose heart and hope."

The CEO should also be mindful colleges contribute to the economic development of communities they serve. Not only should the college employ community members but also form partnerships with businesses, industries, and service organizations within the community in order to contribute to the economic vitality of the area. Numerous grants and other opportunities exist for engaging community entities in partnerships that strengthen both the college and the community.

It is this special connection between community and higher education that makes community colleges unique. Sometimes that connection can be frustrating, but the vitality derived from the connection with the community is what makes community colleges both important institutions in higher education and a critical component in the growth and development of our society at large.

❖

9

Personnel

VINEYARD SYMPOSIUM ISSUES

- Getting the right people on the bus and in the right seats.

  - Training each college executive in the culture of the college and the district and training them in an effort to improve their performance.

  - Removing poor performers when the college has a long history of overlooking their performance in terms of accountability and evaluation.

  - Dealing with internal backlash from terminations and "forced" retirements when the CEO feels they were the right decisions, but some feel they were unjust.

- Improving communication with vice presidents, deans, directors and department chairs. Getting administrators and faculty leaders to own their communication instead of invoking the president's name.

- Attracting and preparing new leaders and providing succession planning.

  - Developing internal leaders.

  - Advancing diversity when it does not exist within the college.

  - Overcoming hiring cynicism from past acts of favoritism and side deals by the previous CEO.

One of the most well-known axioms in management and leadership is that great leaders surround themselves with great people. While that principle seems logical and easy, too many leaders surround themselves with people who are weaker than they are with the hope it will make them look better by comparison. That might even be true, but the overall performance of the leader and the organization will suffer.

Getting the Right People on the Bus

Of course, it is not enough to just select the right people. The leader also needs to be sure all managers are serving in the proper role to maximize their talents. And, even then, the job is not done unless the leader empowers them. This is frequently where the leadership process falls apart. The leader selects good people, puts them in the proper role but does not empower them. In particular, and often out of insecurity, the leader holds on to all the control. Not only will this make the organization less functional, but it will be very unfulfilling for the subordinates. If the leader has truly attracted quality people under these circumstances, they will not stay.

In *Good to Great,* Jim Collins calls this concept "getting the right people on the bus." However, don't forget the other two steps of getting them in the right seats on the bus and empowering them to perform their job in a way that maximizes the organization's utilization of their talents.

An important part of this empowerment is to properly introduce them to the culture of the college and to continually help them improve their performance. It is helpful if every college has some form of introductory orientation for a new employee that explains the culture of the college and the district. As part of that introduction, the CEO should present the history of the college or district, what makes the college or district unique, the CEO's personal goals, and the CEO's personal expectations of new employees. Hearing such information from the CEO sends a positive message to new employees about the CEO's values and communicates to them how important they, as new employees, are to the institution. Part of the goal of the introduction is to define expectations before new employees are influenced by poor performers (minimal workers, negative people, etc.) and follow up with them to keep reinforcing positive qualities. It is equally important that there is also an individual meeting between new employees and their supervisors to clearly define expectations at the individual job level. Unfortunately, sometimes this does not occur at the executive level. CEOs must adequately define for their direct reports the specifics of the job and the expected performance outcomes. It can be difficult to adequately assess job performance if the expectations have not been adequately expressed.

If the CEO has current executives who need training in the culture of the college, engage them as part of the group that develops the introduction so they learn the culture as they design the program. Of course, they could also participate in the program. The biggest issue is attitude. If the executives have a positive attitude toward training, learning about the culture of the college can be easily remedied. If they have a negative attitude and resist training, orientation to the college culture is part of a structured evaluation and remediation program. Furthermore, it is imperative that CEOs participate at some level in the development and execution of the program to be sure it meets their expectations and underscores the importance to the participants.

Another important part of the introduction can be a management-sponsored tour of the facilities and the service area. In multi-college districts, it is particularly important for new employees to know they are becoming part of an organization that is larger than their individual work location. They work *at* a location but *for* a district or system; all employees are working for the success of students. They are part of a larger whole. They should see the parts that make up the whole and the resources available to them. A tour could take an entire day, in some cases, but worth it in the end, for the new employee gets to see the diversity in the system and to meet employees at other locations.

The broader issue of executive leadership development is probably best served elsewhere, but the best places to start are with the specific training provided by statewide organizations such as ACCCA and the chief instructional, business, and student services officers or to find a coach/mentor for leaders who need development.

Moving People on the Bus
The corollary to getting the right people on the bus and in the right seats is to move the wrong people off the bus or to a different seat. There are a number of strategies for helping people who simply need more training or help. However, in this case, the issue is one of trying to remove poor performers when the college has a long history of overlooking their performance in terms of accountability and evaluation. There is nothing to do but to start the process in the way it should have been handled. Ensure that a policy and/or procedure or agreement exists that clearly defines the evaluation process. If one does not exist, create one. If one exists

and has not been followed, implement it. As mentioned previously, that starts with a clear statement of expectations in terms of job performance and expected performance outcomes. It should be emphasized that the institution holds evaluation of its employees as a value designed to enhance performance, improve professionalism, and improve the organization as a whole. Because many employees see evaluation as punitive, it is important to emphasize the positive aspects of evaluation. The first, new evaluation needs to be based on the individual's performance relative to these stated and written expectations. If the first evaluation is negative, it should be mentioned that the performance history was not good, but it was undocumented. Furthermore, the basis for determining that history (at least in general terms) should be included in the evaluation. The point is to make clear that the past silence on performance does not mean approval. How the process proceeds from this point depends on the attitude of the person being evaluated. A genuine interest in improving is different from denial of performance. The reaction determines the course of action. Frequently, when executives understand the current circumstances, they start looking for another job. Helping that person find that job can be the best solution for all parties.

One of the most difficult jobs for most CEOs is to terminate an employee or create a "forced retirement." Every employee has some positive qualities and has made some useful contribution to the college. As a result, no employee is completely incompetent, offensive, and universally viewed as a detriment to the college. That means every employee who is terminated will have supporters who feel the action is not warranted. However, the CEO needs to remember every employee is entitled to a graceful and dignified exit if separating an individual from the institution becomes the only option. Usually, supporters who feel the action is unjust do not know the full set of circumstances, and the CEO cannot tell them because of the privacy rights of the person being terminated. All the CEO can do is indicate it was done in a caring manner and based on all information available. The CEO can also talk about the process so people know the process is fair. However, the CEO usually cannot give the specific justification for the action. At times, it is made even worse because the terminated person may be giving people only partial information or even lies. Nevertheless, the CEO must maintain confidentiality and work with the departing employee in a respectful manner. If necessary, the CEO must face the difficult task of separating an employee from the institution. That task is probably the most difficult of all the challenges of the job, but, occasionally, it must be done.

Communication

Communication problems are frequently discussed at the symposium and throughout this publication. However, sometimes inadequate communication processes and skills are the primary contributors to a personnel problem. Everybody within the organization wants information communicated to them, either directly or indirectly, from the people higher than they are in the organization. At a minimum, employees need to know the information that subordinates or constituents expect them to know as part of their job description. When employees lack that information, they appear foolish and incompetent; this, in turn, can create resentment. At the other end of the spectrum, most people recognize information is power when it exceeds the minimum amount of information to perform one's job. It is up to the CEO to determine how much information beyond "the need to know" is shared with others in the organization.

The CEO's first responsibility is to communicate with the direct reports (including constituent leaders of the faculty, staff, and students). The communication needs to be a combination of group discussion and individual meetings. The frequency of each form of communication and the organization of the groups will vary by the style of the CEO and the structure of the college. The important thing to remember is that, for expediency, it is easy for the CEO to be overly dependent on group communication and neglect giving direct reports individual access. Individual meetings don't have to be frequent, but they must be regular. In the case of direct reports (e.g. vice presidents) in turn communicating with their direct reports (e.g. deans), the plan needs to be developed by the vice president (or corresponding person). It is not the CEO's responsibility to develop a communication plan for them, but it is important to be sure that the communication is occurring. A common failing within a hierarchical organization is that communication is received but not transmitted which leads people to being uniformed or reaching incorrect conclusions. Likewise, it is equally important that CEOs do not go around their direct reports. The CEO should either communicate through the direct reports or in concert with them.

When CEOs diligently communicate through their direct reports, they create a situation in which unpopular messages might cause the direct report to invoke the CEO's name. If the direct report was not consulted, it is at least understandable. However, what the direct reports don't realize is they are telling everyone they have no authority or power and are just a conduit. Contrary to their intentions, they would be better off presenting the message with the relevant reasoning without indicating they were directed to do it. Furthermore, when they invoke the CEO's name, the CEO will form an unflattering opinion of the person and also perceive them as a conduit. This means the CEO may perceive there is no need to involve them in future policy discussions, just give them the decision. The result is that they truly did lose power. As a consequence, CEOs are inappropriately encouraged to bypass their direct reports and deliver the message themselves because they can probably do a better job of representing the logic of the decision. Even when the message is unpopular, employees within the organization enhance their roles when they own the communication by simply delivering the message with the associated reasoning and without invoking the name of anyone higher in the organization. CEOs need to help people within the organization understand this concept. Besides, in many cases, other people within the organization will know the source of the decision even if they have not been named.

Training New Leaders
Community college leadership positions are difficult jobs that are becoming tougher, and the situation is being exacerbated by high turnover rates, partly attributable to an unusual number of retirements from Baby Boomers. While data are not readily available for turnover rates below the vice president level, it is known the median tenure for CEOs in California is three and one-half years, and vice presidents of instruction have experienced annual turnovers in excess of 25 percent. The increases in systemic retirements at all levels from Baby Boomer retirements and the volatility at the CEO and vice president levels has placed a strain on finding available, talented leaders. In response to this problem, many districts have created programs to develop leaders within their own colleges. Two examples are at the Contra Costa Community College District (CCCCD) and the Kern Community College District (KCCD).

The CCCCD program is conducted biennially in spring terms and is designed to provide employees with the opportunity to enhance their understanding of the community college environment and higher education in general. In addition to learning more about the district, participants gain the essential competencies necessary to be academic leaders, administrators, or managers in a community college setting. The program operates on the basic premise that the district's greatest strength has always been its employees, so it is important the district's leadership provides professional growth opportunities so talented staff can enhance their careers for the future.

The Kern Community College District Leadership Academy was initiated to provide a venue for leadership development to employees with at least three years of service and demonstrated leadership acumen in their roles as faculty, classified staff, or management. Applications and references are required. Over the course of nine months, eight day-long structured programs are conducted to prepare a cohort of up to 15 selected employees for professional advancement by providing opportunities for participants to acquire a foundation of knowledge and skills required of college leaders at various levels of the organization. The program includes workshops held at each of the district's three college campuses, conference travel, and team projects that address goals identified in the district's Strategic Plan. Participants develop a greater understanding of the geographically expansive district and build cross-district relationships with co-workers as well as connections with presenters.

There have historically been two flaws with internal programs. First, the wrong people are in the program. People need to participate by invitation so that people who are viewed as having leadership potential are included. It should not be a program in which participants volunteer or just sign-up to participate. Second, in many programs, there is nowhere for "graduates" to go after they complete the program. Developing leadership requires practicing leadership. It might be best to focus internal programs on people who are in some form of leadership already – department chairs, faculty and staff leaders, committee chairs, etc. Training can be small and selective so that you don't just create a group of frustrated people.

Internal leadership programs are also a wonderful means to promote diversity within the management of the college. Because they focus on potential, these programs can provide high potential individuals with the training necessary to level the playing field. However, in general, advancing diversity needs to be a stated priority of the college. More importantly, the value and virtue of diversity, in all its forms, needs to be taught to the college community but on an in-depth level with hiring committees. Each hiring committee needs to include a diversity resource person who reinforces the institutional teachings and who ensures unintended or biased techniques are not imposed on candidate pools, interview grading, and finalist selection. Finding the right resource people is critical. In addition to having a genuine belief in diversity, they also need to be heard by the members of the hiring committee in order to offset unintended bias within some committee members.

Some colleges are plagued by past practices of favoritism and side deals by previous CEOs. When potential applicants become cynical about hiring or selection processes, good candidates may choose not to apply. The only solution is by actions. Insist that all hirings go through a defined process and that each link is connected to the next level. For example, have the department chair (or hiring committee chair) sit with the CEO in the final interviews. Some trusted member of the hiring committee needs to convey that the final process was valid. He or she doesn't necessarily have to participate, but she or he needs to be a full observer so that they can be a legitimate reporter. Too often, a candidate who was a favorite of the committee performs poorly in the final interview and, as a result, is not selected. It is invaluable to have the link to the committee explain the rationale for the decision by the CEO.

One other message is also important to deliver to all applicants. Every selected applicant benefits from being the product of a fair and unbiased process. When the process is short-circuited or perceived to be a case of favoritism, the person selected starts with a problem. That person is not seen as the legitimate "winner" of the process and is viewed with suspicion by the people she or he is trying to lead. Fair processes at least give the person selected the air of legitimacy as he or she starts the new job.

Personnel issues can be one of the most challenging areas of leadership for CEOs. The array of individual problems is enormous, and there is no way a CEO can be trained to handle all of them. At the same time, when the issue is an interpersonal problem involving a college leader, dealing with the issue and the consequences of certain behaviors can consume enormous amounts of the CEO's time. While perhaps not of the same magnitude, selecting or inheriting inappropriate members of the leadership team can also be extremely time consuming. When a CEO has a great leadership team and very few personnel problems, there is a tendency to take the lack of problems as the expected mode of operation. However, once a problem is experienced by CEOs, they never again take harmony and success for granted.

10

Personal Professional Challenges

VINEYARD SYMPOSIUM ISSUES

- Being consumed by daily challenges that keep the president and the college from moving forward. Institutional emotion related to many issues exceeds the substantive importance of the issue, and struggles feed on themselves.

- Finding time to work on the big vision instead of fighting small fires and human resource issues.

- Deciding when a president should leave. Most often it is circumstances like the following:

  - the chancellor is not leaving, and the relationship is unacceptable;

  - a minority portion of the board obstructs progress and is vocal and derisive toward the CEO; and

---

- if CEOs know they have made mistakes, should they look for a new place to receive a second chance or stick it out and try to repair their current circumstances?

- Expanding one's knowledge and network to compensate or correct for certain deficiencies from his or her route to the presidency.

- Avoiding burnout due to the work hours and regaining some balance in one's life.

A CEO's tenure at a college is an evolution in which personal and professional issues change as the CEO cycles through the different stages. While there are probably many different stages depending on the CEO and the college, there are at least three stages. The first stage is when CEOs are new to a college and are attempting to establish themselves as the leader of the institution and trying to connect with the people within the college community. This is an incredibly time-consuming stage because the CEO needs to be physically present as much as possible on the campus (and at college events) and in the community. Many CEOs will tell you there is not much time for a personal life in this first stage. However, if CEOs successfully emerge from the first phase, they are well positioned for the second stage, which is usually the stage that provides the greatest stability in the CEO's tenure and the greatest opportunity for leading the college. The third stage is where the CEO has the greatest flexibility. If the first two stages have been successful, the college trusts the CEO, listens to the CEO, and knows the CEO. This environment gives the CEO the chance to define the final stage of his or her tenure at the college. CEOs can usually reduce their physical presence at events, and the college is supportive of greater CEO involvement outside the college (either in state or local college organizations or local community activities). It can also be a dangerous time for CEO tenure. By this stage, the CEO has made many decisions that, by necessity, offended certain individuals. Also, a segment of the college community tires of a CEO's idiosyncrasies. It is why a CEO must also know when it is time to leave.

If CEOs do not successfully complete each phase, they can cycle through these stages in less than five years. It is why the median tenure for a CEO in California is three and one-half years. However, even successful CEOs will often cycle through the stages in ten years and really need to consider the next chapter of their career or life. There is nothing worse than watching successful CEOs overstay their tenure. Of course there are exceptions, and there are CEOs who have successful tenures over 20 years at the same college. Those are aberrations and are the result of a unique relationship among a CEO, a board of trustees, and a college as well as a unique desire by the CEO to stay in the same job for that length of time.

CEOs have a classic dilemma – long-term responsibility within college environments that are focused on the short term. Community college cultures are products of our national culture which is a short-term culture. Politicians are worried about being reelected or elected for a new job and often only care about results within their term of office. Investors press boards of directors and CEOs of corporations for short-term profits to boost stock prices. As a society, we have a harder time with voluntarily saving for retirement versus satisfying current wants. That same mentality exists inside a college – especially when it is usually the case that every short-term problem has not been solved. The CEO has to break that cycle and encourage people to spend some of the institutional energy on a longer term vision. To do that, he or she must convince people the long-term vision matters (and help people understand the consequences of just looking at the short term) and that the outcomes of a long-term vision are meaningful and will be acted upon. Sometimes it is easier for the CEO to start with financial issues because they are concrete (unless this is an area of controversy). For example, a long-term vision is important when it focuses on the need to build reserves or to find solutions to unfunded liabilities (retiree health plans) or to resolve a structural deficit. A CEO must start by looking for long-term topics upon which everyone can agree (in-house leadership development, succession planning, and maintenance of recently built buildings). In the case of the maintenance issue, the CEO can show what happened when deferred maintenance was neglected in order to balance the current budget. The CEO needs to show that being consumed in the petty and the immediate is keeping the college from dealing with the important, big issues. It is not that the college won't continue to work on those immediate issues, but it won't be all consuming and worked on at the expense of dealing with long-term concerns. The CEO should also recognize one of the reasons institutions fail to focus on long-term, big issues is that it is easier to debate or argue over the minor or petty issues. These issues don't require the same level of thought, arguments don't need to be structured rationally, there is far more certainty in people's minds as to what is right, and the motivation is often selfish because the outcome directly affects the person.

Even when an institution demonstrates a willingness to work on long-term problems and issues, CEOs themselves have to find the time to work on the major issues instead of being consumed in daily operating problems. CEOs need to find some method for carving out their own time without closing themselves off from the people in the college. In other words, don't start closing the door and say don't interrupt me. Instead, find a way to think outside the office. Many CEOs do some of their best thinking while going on walks alone. CEOs can schedule walks in which part of the time is a walk around campus talking with people, and part of the time is walking alone. These walk times should be scheduled and hold as much priority as any other meeting. People seem to be very accepting of this practice because many employees see and interact with the CEO during a portion of the walk.

Beyond the walks, CEOs should find a place on campus outside their office where they can go to write. For some, it might be a study booth in the corner of the library. Not only does everyone leave the CEO alone because they could not find the CEO (and besides, writing in a library is perceived to be serious work), but the CEO also frequently has a chance to interact with students. The other time that is available is at the beginning and end of the day. CEOs work long hours, but it is usually quiet before 8:00 a.m. in the morning and after 6:00 p.m. in the evening. While these are just examples of carving out time to work on a vision or long-term issues, it is important every CEO find a comparable way to have time to think, create, and reflect. To be a leader, a CEO must be more than just a solver of operating problems.

Knowing When to Leave

One of the most difficult personal decisions for a CEO is knowing when to leave a position. Ironically, it can be an equally complex decision for the CEO who has had a very successful and lengthy tenure at a college as it can be for a CEO who is struggling due to a conflict with the chancellor or the board or the college at large. In the case of a CEO completing a successful, lengthy tenure, the first concern is "staying too long at the fair." Many successful leaders have trouble leaving their jobs, especially at the end of their careers. Sometimes it is a reluctance to retire, sometimes it is a reluctance to start over in a new job, sometimes it is comfort in the current job, and sometimes it is just completing one more challenge. One common theory is that ten years is about the maximum time a person should stay in the same job. At the end of ten years, the person has probably exhausted his or her contribution, and he or she may have become a leader who is simply maintaining the status quo. When a CEO stays beyond ten years, an organization's culture may have started to stagnate and become too ingrained in a single mode of operation and leadership. Inevitably, even the image of what had been a very effective leader starts to tarnish which also means the person's legacy is tarnished. The second concern is that, even for a successful CEO, when the organizational environment changes and is no longer a good fit for the person, it is time to leave. The common mistake is the belief that the accumulative goodwill created by a successful tenure will carry the CEO through a bad fit. It will not. For the successful CEO, knowing when to leave is important, both for the CEO and the college. If circumstances and the position of the CEO are allowed to deteriorate, it will inevitably cause conflict and dissent within the college as people split between protecting the CEO and others calling for change.

It is equally difficult for a CEO to decide to leave when the problem is focused on a conflict with the chancellor in a multi-college district or with an assertive minority group of the board of trustees. If an unresolvable conflict exists between a college president and a district chancellor, and the chancellor has indicated he or she is not leaving, the only choice for the president is to leave. If the college president goes around the chancellor to the board, it usually fails or creates a "winner takes all" conflict. Most chancellors survive because they have the support of the board majority. If they do not, their days are numbered, and the situation will resolve itself without the college president having to do anything. Even if the chancellor does not have majority support in a specific conflict with a college president, but does have it in terms of the chancellor's job security, the college president might win the battle but has created an untenable working relationship in the long-term that will hurt both the president and the college. The gamble and the resulting conflict is not worth it. It is better to leave. There is one other price that college presidents who create this conflict will pay - boards and chancellors at other colleges will be reluctant to hire them, even if they are talented.

When a college president or district chancellor has to work with a split board of trustees in which the minority group blocks progress and is derisive to the CEO, it makes for an unacceptable work environment for the CEO. First, it is the responsibility of the board majority to control the board minority, at least in terms of civility and decorum. If the emotion can be drained from the conflicts, it is much easier to deal with the different policy positions. Unfortunately, the CEO is not in a position to help modify this behavior. If the board majority cannot do it, outside assistance should be sought. Besides the usual consultants, the board might consider bringing in someone whom the entire board will respect (e.g. a retired, successful elected official). Second, is there any chance on the horizon for a change in the board composition? If it might improve in a relatively short time, the CEO can decide if it is worth waiting it out. Third, the CEO should consider leaving. The usual dilemma is that the CEO feels beholden to the board majority and that leaving allows the minority to win. However, if the majority cannot control the minority and there has been no success in changing the minority's behavior, the CEO certainly has a license to leave. No CEO wants to be miserable all the time, and it does not make sense to stay if the situation is incurable.

The final situation in which a CEO needs to consider leaving is when a CEO has made mistakes, and a significant portion of the college community is unhappy with their performance. The real question is whether or not the situation is reparable. It probably matters if the CEO has had a successful tenure at the college prior to the mistakes or if the CEO is new to the college. In both cases, the CEO needs to consult privately with college leaders to see if correction is possible. It is probably worth trying no matter what because an effort to correct the situation may help attain the next job at another college if it becomes necessary. Usually, the ability to correct mistakes depends on the college community's perception (including the board of trustees) of whether the mistakes were an anomaly or part of a regular pattern of behavior.

Expanding a New CEO's Knowledge

Most CEOs assume their first presidency through one of the traditional vice president positions – instruction (or academic affairs), student services (or student affairs), or administrative services (or business). Some CEOs are lucky to have come from an executive vice president position so they have gained knowledge and skills in more than one area. However, in most cases, CEOs assume their first presidency lacking in knowledge in one or more areas. Over the first six months, new CEOs need to be honest in their assessment of their abilities and detail the areas in which they lack knowledge. How they close that gap depends on their own comfort in admitting their shortcomings in their relationships within the college. One solution is to have the vice presidents inside the college teach the CEO about their respective area of expertise. This has the benefit of creating a unique connection with those individuals, and it gives the CEO a unique opportunity to assess each vice president (if appropriate, this could be extended to other positions within the organization). Another method, and perhaps a good starting place, is for the CEO to request participation in the workshops provided for new vice presidents. For example, if the new CEO was a chief student services officer, he or she could request to participate in the training provided by the CIOs and the CBOs. Each organization usually provides a training session for a new vice president (academic affairs, student affairs, and business), and this training would give a CEO an excellent background for each of these silos. Again, the CEO would need to be comfortable requesting the training and to go through it with vice presidents. Beyond that, the new CEO can look for training opportunities at conferences or specific CEO training provided by organizations like the Community College League of California or the American Association of Community Colleges. Finally, if the board of trustees is supportive, the new CEO should consider engaging a coach or mentor who would both provide individualized training and direct the CEO to other training opportunities.

Achieving Balance

CEOs are selected because they have been successful in their former jobs. Often, a key part of that success is due to hard work and long hours. When people work all the time, they receive enormous praise from everyone around them at work while their family and friends tend to accept it as the reality of their job. As someone progresses up the "leadership ladder" to the CEO position, the time demands become greater, and the job becomes more isolating. That is why it is important to determine work boundaries as a CEO because there is a tendency to repeat prior behaviors or exaggerate them - especially if CEOs feel the amount of time spent on the job caused their success. CEOs also need to continually revisit the question of boundaries as their life changes (health issues, family needs, children, and grandchildren) and the length of tenure in the same position changes. All leadership positions require more time at the outset (especially for CEOs), but if the boundary question is not revisited, CEOs will simply expand the job to the available hours as they gain maturity in the job. CEOs also need to assess their productivity by asking whether spending 12 hours a day instead of spending 11 hours a day is really making a significant and meaningful difference.

Setting boundaries is the first step in trying to determine how to stay balanced (physically, spiritually, socially, and emotionally) when the demands of the CEO job "sucks you dry." A CEO's job is never done. There is always something else CEOs can do to make their organization better. The challenge for CEOs is how to create space to meet all their personal needs while doing the best possible job as a leader. It starts by taking an inventory of how CEOs are spending their time. There are limits and places where spending more time on the job does not make a significant difference, especially in light of the toll it takes on the leader. The challenge is discovering where those limits are for the CEO and setting the appropriate boundary. It will also change during the life of the job because the time commitment is greater during the first two years as a CEO when the learning curve is the steepest and the college community is learning about the CEO.

CEOs cannot achieve balance without periodically assessing their use of time and setting boundaries and limits that fit their personal needs. Every CEO is different in terms of the desired balance in his or her life, so there is no magic formula. However, every CEO needs to go through this process on a regular basis and make conscious decisions about boundaries and limits to insure the resulting balance is a conscious, personal decision and is not action by default. Longevity in the CEO job requires some level of acceptable balance is achieved, and it can only happen through a deliberate effort by the CEO. Furthermore, most boards of trustees recognize the importance of CEOs creating boundaries to achieve life balance and will be supportive of the effort once the CEO has completed the first stage of his or her tenure. This is one of the critical areas in which there needs to be stated expectations and a working partnership between the board and the CEO.

APPENDICES

APPENDIX A

Working With The Board Chair

In your CEO role, your major responsibility is to implement policy decisions of the board. Because of the rules and regulations regarding Board meetings and communication between and among board members, you will be required to form a working relationship with the board chair that may differ from your relationship and contact with other board members. The board chair becomes your connection to the board as a whole.

The board chair is responsible to the college/district, other board members, the CEO, and the college/district employees. In fulfilling the CEO role, you should meet regularly with the board chair to provide any support needed in fulfilling the role and to make known particular challenges where the board chair may be able to assist the CEO, especially between board meetings. In the case of a new chair, the CEO may need to provide orientation to the position. Be as helpful as possible in ensuring the board chair is able to fulfill the responsibilities of the position in the following six areas.

1. ENSURE EFFECTIVE TRUSTEESHIP

Board Chair Role

It is the obligation of the board chair to ensure the entire board practices effective trusteeship. Trustees are most effective when they remain in their policy-setting "lane" by relegating responsibility and authority to the CEO to implement and administer board policies without interference and when they operate on the principle of "no surprises." Trustees are to be knowledgeable of their code of conduct and policies governing their behavior and to be respectful of the important principle that the CEO works only for the board as a whole. It is the duty of the board chair to ensure all board members are mindful of their responsibility to not make "end runs" that bypass the administration and to make all board members aware that college constituencies, the public, and even board members work through the CEO, including making complaints and suggestions. Ultimately, it is the board chair who sets the example of professional behavior in all situations.

CEO Role

Work with the board chair to establish training and other resources for board members so that they understand their role. Encourage regular review of the board's code of conduct and other documents that govern board behavior. Emphasize, as appropriate, the CEO role as "implementer" of policies approved by the board and the board's role of setting policy.

2. PROTECTION OF THE COLLEGE/DISTRICT AND THE CEO

<u>Board Chair Role</u>
The board chair should work with fellow board members and the CEO in a spirit of harmony and cooperation, ensuring decisions are based on what is best for the college/district and the students and not on special or personal interests. S/he protects the mission of the college(s) and the long-term interests of the district. Further, it is the board chair who protects the college/district, other board members, and the CEO by avoiding public criticism of the CEO by the board (and vice versa), by holding the CEO accountable, and by being the point of contact for internal board conflicts.

<u>CEO Role</u>
Ensure the board chair and board members have objective information required for good decision making. Do not attempt to solve issues between and among board members. Leave that to the board chair.

3. COMMUNICATION

<u>Board Chair Role</u>
The board chair is responsible for engaging in regular communication with the CEO and board members as allowed by the Brown Act. It is imperative the board chair

maintain excellent communications with the CEO and board members, serving as a sounding board, maintaining confidentiality, and being a good listener. To ensure excellent communication, the board chair should establish an environment (ground rules) so that the CEO does not have to respond to individual board member agendas; be open, forthright, fair, and honest in his/her dealings; and offer support, counsel, and comfort to the CEO.

CEO Role
Establish regular meetings with the board chair. Encourage establishment of a communication protocol for the board so that communication mechanisms are clear.

4. RECOGNIZING BOARD MEMBERS, THE CEO AND OTHER DISTRICT/COLLEGE EMPLOYEES

Board Chair Role
It is the responsibility of the board chair to make sure regular evaluations and reviews of the CEO's contract are conducted in order to ensure provisions are fair and competitive in addition to ensuring regular evaluations of the board. S/he has a duty to advocate for professional development of the CEO, board members, and other college employees and to acknowledge accomplishments of board members and district/college employees in public settings.

CEO Role
Work with the board chair to ensure a policy and procedure are developed for the evaluation of the CEO and board as

well as a calendar of activities to be reviewed annually by the board to ensure appropriate actions are taken. Apprise the board chair of professional activities available for the board and the CEO, and make such information part of board discussions so that commitments can be made. Advocate for budgeting of professional development funds for board members and employees.

5. EFFECTIVE LEADERSHIP

Board Chair Role
The board chair is most effective as a presiding officer when s/he assists the CEO in development of the board agenda; meets with the CEO prior to the meeting to review the board agenda; ensures board members understand how to place items on the agenda; and maintains competence in Robert's Rules of Order and the Brown Act.

The board chair provides leadership in the hiring and departure of the CEO by ensuring CEO changes are planned, orderly, and respectful. S/he ensures a dignified exit of a CEO and plays a leading role in the search for a new CEO, welcoming and orienting the new CEO, and initiating activities to ensure the success of the new CEO.

CEO Role
Meet with the board chair prior to each meeting to review the board agenda. Encourage board training on effective meetings.

6. AUTHORITY AND CREDIBILITY

Board Chair Role

The board chair should realize the extent of his/her authority, recognizing that s/he is but one member of the board, with no more power than another board member. It is the responsibility of the board chair to provide formal direction for the CEO, not that of a single trustee. The effective board chair does not abuse the power s/he has and does not perceive him/herself to be a co- or super-CEO. The credible board chair is open, forthright, even-handed, and trustworthy. S/he maintains confidentiality (personal and personnel); avoids using board meetings and events for personal attention, agendas, or publicity; and sets an example for board philanthropy. It helps if the board chair has a sense of humor.

CEO Role

Seek direction from the board chair, being mindful of the roles. Encourage, as appropriate, professional development that exposes the board chair to appropriate behavior to ensure credibility in the chair role.

*The majority of the content in this document is taken from material presented by the Board Chair Workshop sponsored by the Community College League of California.

APPENDIX B

Survival And Success Tips

For a long time, the League has sponsored a workshop for new CEOs. The workshop is conducted by experienced CEOs that often change every year. In recent years, each CEO panelist is asked to provide their suggestions on survival and success for a new CEO. Here is a sampling of those lists of suggestions with the CEO's title at the time of their presentation. When presented in the workshop, each item was accompanied by an explanation by the CEO. However, even without the explanations, there is wisdom in the lists!

- **HELEN BENJAMIN, CHANCELLOR, CONTRA COSTA COMMUNITY COLLEGE DISTRICT**

  - Admit, analyze, and benefit from your failures/mistakes.
  - Do not seek recognition. If you are doing a good job, your work will be acknowledged by others.
  - Avoid relationships that do not bring you joy.
  - Regardless of the task you have to perform, find joy in it.
  - Take risks!

- Give your time, extraordinary talents, and financial resources to the college/district.
- Grow professionally, intellectually, and emotionally. Regarding the latter, never, ever whine at work. Do that with your therapist.
- Do not wear your race, gender, ethnicity, or feelings on your sleeve!
- Be a quick change artist—adapt to whatever circumstance/ situation in which you find yourself.
- Never, ever lie!

• BYRON CLIFT BRELAND, PRESIDENT, SAN JOSE CITY COLLEGE

- Get to know the "plank owners" or the unofficial leaders of the institution – they can really help you move things without taking a "big hit."
- Talk less and listen more (this really is hard for leaders to do).
- Success ultimately depends on your ability to enlist voluntary commitment rather than the forced obedience of others (giving orders can be costly).
- Learn the culture of the institution and then use it to advance student success efforts.
- Know the difference between a response and a reaction.
- Make time in your schedule for exercise, worship, etc. (act like a president, and take control of your schedule).
- Work to make life better for all stakeholders by leading efforts to improve administrative work processes.
- Encourage people to try new things, and make it OK to fail.
- Lead efforts to improve teaching and learning at the institution.

- Maintain regular communication with the chancellor or the board (your boss), and have no surprises.
- Have a convincing vision (be a champion for student success).
- Learn to manage organizational context rather than focus on daily operations.
- Stay informed of state and national legislation efforts.
- Remember that enthusiasm and fun are important – when you have fun, you can do a great job!

• BEN DURAN, SUPERINTENDENT/PRESIDENT, MERCED COLLEGE

- Display integrity – Say who you are and be who you say.
- Hire smart – Surround yourself with really smart and competent people.
- Make allies.
- Stay physically and mentally healthy.
- Know your finances.
- Be visible and available.
- Get involved in your community.
- Manage large changes or shifts through your office.
- Keep board members on speed dial.
- Hire a law firm you trust.

• NICKI HARRINGTON, CHANCELLOR, YUBA COMMUNITY COLLEGE DISTRICT

- Have a sense of humor. Ask yourself: "How important is it?"
- Know yourself.

- Don't compromise your values.
- Have a vision but be open to new ideas.
- Me "in the role," not me "the person"
- Have a trusted colleague (not family) in whom you can confide and who will identify your flawed thinking.
- Sharpen the saw:
  - Physical
  - Mental
  - Emotional/Social
  - Spiritual
- Don't sweat the small stuff, but do sweat the details.
- Always do your homework for all groups.
- Balance your networking.
  - Internal vs. External.
  - Board vs. faculty and staff.
- Build a strong team – those who challenge your thinking, but not divisive; ongoing development.
- Modeling, mentoring, mattering:
  - Always the mentor, always the mentee.
  - Know your weaknesses, and actively work on improvement.

- **CINDY MILES, CHANCELLOR, GROSSMONT-CUYAMACA COMMUNITY COLLEGE DISTRICT**

  - Learn to read, honor, and work with the existing culture.
  - If you don't listen, they stop talking.
  - Invest in engaging the board as your partner.
  - Remember your TREASURE = Students! (Find ways to stay connected to learning core.)
  - Take on the FULL mantle of leadership (You EMBODY the institution and the COMMON VISION – you _ARE_ the BRAND).

- Call out the GOODNESS in everyone – people hunger for HIGHER PURPOSE….call out their higher angels.
- Don't let the "DAILY CRAZIES" obscure your STRATEGIC Direction.
- Find THINK TIME.
- Identify your TOUCHSTONES and TRUTHTELLERS – and use them.

Always remember: this is a RELATIONSHIP business.

• KINDRED MURILLO, SUPERINTENDENT/ PRESIDENT, LAKE TAHOE COMMUNITY COLLEGE

- Stay focused on students when making decisions, not just a few students but all students. Students are why we exist, and I never lose sight of that.
- Tenacity pays off. Assess your current reality, create a clear vision, and put the steps in place to make the vision a reality. Have the tenacity to keep moving.
- Have the courage to do what is right. Courage is the toughest lesson, with the biggest payoff. Have the courage to do the right thing for the entire institution.
- It is not necessary to react, and discernment is essential. Never react, but make sure you use discernment to ensure you follow up on essential items.
- Ensure you have the right people. There is nothing more powerful than a team of highly motivated, ethical leaders moving toward a common goal.
- Take responsibility. Taking responsibility is important to the growth and development of your team. Admit your mistakes.

- Listen and have compassion. People need to be heard. Listening and understanding conveys that you care about staff, faculty, and students.
- Set high expectations, and nurture your team to meet those expectations. Do not accept mediocrity; the goal is continuous improvement, not perfection.
- Check yourself at the door. Self-awareness is essential. Never lose sight as the CEO; you are responsible for the entire organization and for your actions.

Know when to trust and when to intervene. Trust is good, although when your gut tells you to dig deeper, or there is something wrong, pay attention and act.

• SANDRA SERRANO, CHANCELLOR, KERN COMMUNITY COLLEGE DISTRICT

- Develop relationships.
- Listen with interest, and ask questions.
- Keep your eyes and ears open to what is happening.
- Everyone wants a decision; be decisive and timely.
- Have the courage to do the right thing.
- It is okay to say, "I don't know" or "I made an error."
- Set the example, leadership matters/
- Confront performance problems/
- Engage in state associations and local organizations.

Communicate, communicate, communicate.

• GIL STORK, SUPERINTENDENT/PRESIDENT, CUESTA COLLEGE

- Demonstrate a passion for what you do and the privilege to serve as a CEO.
- Take time to size up the competency of your leadership team, and make changes when necessary.
- Get to know each trustee individually, and establish a clear understanding with the board of trustees as to your authority to run the college.
- Establish a regular, standing meeting with constituent leaders.
- Create an opportunity for the campus community to hear from you on important issues, and provide the opportunity for the campus community to ask questions.
- Video as many campus events, presentations, programs as possible and make them available to both internal and external audiences. Promotes transparency.
- Create multiple "faces" of the college ....Not only the president's.
- Establish a close working relationship with the district's K-12 superintendents.
- Work towards establishing an integrated planning process that is viewed as "President Proof."
- Commit sufficient time and energy to advancement efforts of the college to generate significant financial and friend support.

Be visible…on campus…in the community.

- **LINDA THOR, CHANCELLOR, FOOTHILL-DE ANZA COMMUNITY COLLEGE DISTRICT**

  - Never get crossways with the faculty; if you think the faculty are the enemy, resign.
  - Perception is more important than reality; learn the importance of symbolism.
  - Explain, explain, explain and then explain some more.
  - Be a cheerleader – instill a sense of pride and ownership among employees.
  - Ask for and listen to suggestions – the people who do the work know best how to improve the work; allow yourself to be influenced.
  - Learn the culture and honor the history of the institution before you make major changes; you can renew an institution, but you can't change its past.
  - Remember that it takes longer to mend fences than it does to touch bases.
  - Trust your intuition, your gut.
  - Never cover up illegal or unethical activity; keep your integrity in tack!

Be open as a person – if they like and admire you, they will have trust and confidence in you.

- **DEBBIE TRAVIS, PRESIDENT, COSUMNES RIVER COLLEGE**

  - Build a diverse and resilient team; plan for systematic development; and welcome spontaneous opportunities for growth.
  - Talk to colleagues about what they value (learn the hidden rules and protocols of the college).

- Be open and clear with your vision, values, and concerns.
- Be accessible and visible at the college and in the community; invite colleagues from all constituencies to join you at internal and external events.
- Verify data before important decisions and always check your decisions and strategic plans for "blind spots."
- Provide "holding environments" for brainstorming new efforts and problem-solving issues impacting the college.
- Develop the ability to tell a good story and keep a journal. Someone once said, "writing is a profound way to codify one's thoughts," and it is also therapeutic.
- Do your homework and be prepared for meetings, presentations, discussions, and impromptu speeches.
- Never underestimate the power of an appreciative comment or an apology.

Adopt the perspective that leadership is learning and teaching, an ever-changing, daily continuum requiring knowledge, integrity, patience, compassion, grace, and laughter.

• ROCKY YOUNG, CHANCELLOR (RETIRED), LOS ANGELES COMMUNITY COLLEGE DISTRICT

- Leadership is about using your influence, not the authority associated with your position. If you use your power, you lose your power.
- One-half of one percent of any group causes the problems – students, faculty, and community. Maintain perspective in the face of critics or complainers.
- Be prepared for all leadership situations (speeches, meetings, etc.). Frequently, people judge you as knowledgeable

and competent simply because you were prepared. First impressions matter; for many, it is their only impression.

- Leadership traits need to be internalized so that you are using genuine beliefs and feelings.
- Surround yourself with great leaders – hopefully, better than you. Empower them. Hear their idea before you give your opinions. Make sure the people who work for you know you care about them, both professionally and personally.
- Be accessible. Part of being trusted and people feeling connected to you is through casual interaction. Don't close your door, and walk around.
- Know which "hills you are willing to die on." You cannot have too many, and you should keep it to yourself.
- Transparency breeds trust. Be honest, admit your mistakes, and genuinely share credit.
- Don't fear failure. Encourage others to make suggestions and take risks. If you agree and do it, and it is successful, give them credit. If it fails, take the blame because you are the one who decided to go ahead with the idea. Create a climate that welcomes and listens to new ideas.
- Your biggest responsibility is to instill hope and optimism within the organization.
- A leader is always teaching, whether it is sharing knowledge, explaining a situation, or helping people to understand your decisions.

APPENDIX C

Advice For Succeeding In Challenging Times
Asilomar Leadership Skills Seminar

Helen Benjamin, Cindy Miles, Thelma Scott-Skillman, and Sandra Serrano

1. Listen to understand.
2. Listen to your gut – respect your integrity and your ethics.
3. Encourage discussion. Then listen.
4. Watch. Be observant.
5. Manage your emotions, and be calm.
6. Demonstrate self-confidence.
7. Be decisive (but not reactive) and timely.
8. Be willing to change.
9. Flow with ambiguity.
10. Think analytically.
11. Think globally.
12. Recognize trends.
13. Build relationships.
14. Avoid relationships that do not bring you joy.

15. Understand and embrace politics.
16. Study organizational culture – culture eats strategy for breakfast!
17. Be approachable.
18. Be nice. Do *not* be a brillo pad.
19. Be a learner – expand your knowledge base.
20. Understand finance and budgets.
21. Become engaged in committees and arenas beyond your comfort zone.
22. Find joy in your work (or find new work☺).
23. Be passionate.
24. Define who you are.
25. Know and accept the obligation that comes with leadership.
26. Work hard.
27. Be patient.
28. Take the long view.
29. Grow professionally.
30. Take risks.
31. Expect and accept constructive criticism.
32. Analyze and, therefore, benefit from your failures.
33. Volunteer in the community.
34. Give.
35. Do not wear your race, gender, or ethnicity on your sleeve!
36. Have fun!

APPENDIX D

Leadership Blues

*L*eadership Blues was an opinion piece written, in part, by Steve Weiner (one of the founders of the Vineyard Symposium). It is nearly 15 years old, and might be slightly outdated, but it is sent to symposium participants for their reading as a means to stimulate their thinking about their presidency.

After reading *Leadership Blues*, or before, each participant is asked, "What's waking you up at night?" While it is recognized that each participant is facing challenging leadership roles, the facilitators know some issues are more worrisome than others. Given about two weeks, it is requested that each participant email the other participants and the facilitators a one-two page summary of his or her current leadership challenge(s). Everyone is reminded that all communications are **strictly confidential** and for current Vineyard Symposium participants only! This exercise starts to set the tone for the symposium before the participants arrive in Napa.

Leadership Blues
Revised October 2, 2002
James G. March and Stephen S. Weiner

A few months before the end of the Second World War, General Tomoyuki Yamashita of the Imperial Japanese Army was sent to the Philippines to take command of the Japanese army there. The military situation was impossible, and within a few months General Yamashita surrendered. One month later, on command of General Douglas MacArthur he was brought before an American military tribunal.[3] The military officers heard testimony that troops under General Yamashita's command had committed atrocities in the Philippines during the final campaign in the islands. The general and his American defense lawyers argued that his army was so disorganized by the attack of allied forces that he did not know of the atrocities and that he could not have done anything about them ever if he had known.

Why was General Yamashita brought before the military tribunal? Perhaps it was because he failed to prevent atrocities. Perhaps it was because he had led an attacking force of 30,000 men overland down the Malay Peninsula to capture Singapore and its defending army of 100,000 men early in the war. Perhaps it was because there was anger toward the Japanese in the United States and in the Philippines, and someone had to become a focus for that anger. Perhaps it was because his trial could be a symbol and trophy of General MacArthur's personal power.

It is not easy to make any clear historical assertion about why General Yamashita was brought before the tribunal. But it is not hard to see his experience as a metaphor for the way the joys and angers of others are displaced upon leaders. It is a fundamental

---

[3] In 1949, one of General Yamashita's defense lawyers published a book detailing the story of these proceedings. See A. Frank Reel, *The Case of General Yamashita*. Chicago, IL: University of Chicago Press, 1949.

reality of leadership that it reaps the rewards of public satisfaction and bears the blame for public unhappiness. It matters rather little whether a leader has done much to create the former or could have done much to prevent the latter. The necessity of social attribution of leader responsibility is an article of faith and an instinct of social behavior. The reputations of all leaders are variations on the reputations of generals.

College and university presidents are not subject to court-martial nor are they in danger of being executed. But a surprisingly large number feel they have been victims of capricious cruelty at least once in their careers. We have spent a not inconsiderable portion of our professional lives listening to presidential tales of distress and anxiety; of coping with unexpected turbulence in presidential lives; of struggling with crises for which presidents were ill-prepared and over which they had scant control.

These stories, and the painful experiences that give rise to them, are what we call the "Leadership Blues." One hears these Blues not in the confines of a well-upholstered office during business hours but, rather, over a bottle of wine late in the evening, or during a long walk on a sandy beach, or in the midst of a transcontinental plane flight.

Not all presidents sing the Blues but the odds go up dramatically as the years of presidential tenure increase.

Hearing the Blues stir chords of memory among those who have attempted leadership in similar settings because they capture recurring, important, and often unpleasant features of administrative life in academic organizations. The underlying importance of the Blues is what they say about campus culture, about civility, and about the pleasures and penalties of leadership roles in contemporary colleges. As these matters exert heavy influence over the character of those attracted or repelled by the task of campus leadership, they raise serious questions for American higher education and the society that they serve. We want to understand the Blues and, in a later section, to spell out some implications for community college leadership.

The Blues arise from experiences that either end a presidency or come close to it:

- A president, facing major budgetary problems, proposes to sell some rarely used athletic practice fields to a corporation in search of space to build. The proposal stirs keen opposition and the resulting firefight features an Athletic Department, prominent alumni and several student groups on the attack.

- A new president, thinking she has the mandate to organize her office as she sees fit, decides to transfer a presidential assistant, who is Latina, to a job in student services. Shortly after, the disgruntled employee files suit to reverse the transfer and the campus erupts amidst charges of insensitivity and presidential racism.

- At a public college with a collective bargaining agreement with faculty, a president struggles to conclude negotiations over a new contract. The faculty union persists in salary demands that the president believes are far beyond the capacity of the college to pay. The president does not budge and the faculty vote "no confidence" in the president. The president turns to his board of trustees for support and discovers that the board majority is beholden to the union because of past contributions to their election campaigns.

- A president, seeking to save money on a building project that is over budget, asks his wife, a professional architect, to volunteer her services to trim the project budget. She carries out her task but with little sense of diplomacy. Veteran college officials, believing that the president's action disregards their professional qualifications, deeply resent this intrusion into their domain. The campus is seized by allegations of presidential favoritism and micromanagement and staff morale sinks.

- A president announces the single largest unrestricted gift in the history of her college. As soon as the president decides on the allocation of the gift, a broad campus coalition organizes to oppose the president's decision as arbitrary and made without proper consultation on campus. The coalition demands an audience with the board of trustees in public session.

- A president suffers under the continuing, bitter criticism of a leading member of the board of trustees. The trustee finds no presidential recommendation or decision worthy of support and puts out the word that disaffected members of the college community can bring grievances directly to him. He collects many complaints quickly, in part because of his reputation as the person responsible for the firing of a previous president.

In each of the foregoing cases, and this is but a small sample, the resulting travail lasted for months or years. And, to be sure, each of these incidents triggered a conflagration because previous events had provided some tinder for the blaze. But, for each of the presidents involved, the crisis came as a shock.

Of course, like the story of General Yamashita as told by his lawyer, the Blues we have heard come only from the president's point of view. Other people who were involved would tell different stories speaking of different motivations, intentions and outcomes. Specific events or encounters would read differently if told from another angle of observation. For example, college trustees often play a role in the Blues and, when they do, the presidential perspective colors the offending trustees with hues of brashness, personal enmity, ideological passion, and/or simple political ambition. The trustees would undoubtedly provide a different account that speaks of accountability to the governing board and the difficulties of making entrenched bureaucracies respond.

For anyone who has not endured similar experiences, expressions of pain by leaders might be seen as out of keeping with the old cliché about what happens when the going gets tough, or as some kind of sour grapes on the part of those who have been left behind by a competitive world. Such an impression would, however, be misleading. One usually does not hear the Blues from the losers in administrative life. It is the survivors who live to sing the Blues. In some cases, they have survived by dogged persistence, in some cases because their opponents lost interest in the attack, in other cases by leaving one field of battle for a fresh one on another campus. But they have survived. Their pains are not the excuses of losers but the laments of survivors, laments for a lost dream of an idyllic academic institution at least as seen by a president.

The Blues are full of outrage and hurt. Presidents who sing the Blues expected something different. And they expected something better. They anticipated hard work, making tough decisions and experiencing unpopularity in their professional roles. Leaders of academic institutions have to be ready for such difficulties. They face the challenges posed by the irreverence and indifference of students, the resistance of faculty members who prize their individual and collective autonomy, and the challenges of board members trying to establish their own authority. The college campus has never been an easy place for administrators. But presidents with the Blues got far more pain than they bargained for.

Leaders with the Blues have encountered worlds that typically contain four features that run through the stories they tell: First, the issues that they confronted were contested with fervor, but they were usually not major issues of educational policy. The outcomes of campus struggles certainly involve short-term political advantage and some redistribution of power and influence on college campuses, the ebb and flow of careers and fights over keeping and losing jobs

We learn from the Blues that loss of employee morale or trustee confidence is a likely ticket out of town for an administrator, whereas instructional effectiveness, a stale curriculum, or anemic graduation or student transfer rates can often be lost in the noise of campus politics. There are relatively few fights over criteria for faculty hiring or promotion, deep changes in the structure of curricula or substantial alterations in expectations for student performance. The fundamental educational character of the college is rarely at issue (noteworthy exceptions to this rule are attempts to admit men to women's colleges or women to all-male colleges.) The most common feature of the conflicts reflected in the Blues appears to be jostling for primacy among small groups or individuals or the bumping of one set of career expectations against other career paths.

Second, the level of anger and emotion involved in the encounters is out of all proportion to the substantive importance of the issues to which they are explicitly addressed. The criticism voiced by the opposition may be out in the open or it may be carried in rumors or whispered comments. Presidents are in positions of formal authority (no matter how shaky they may feel) and their enemies, fearful of the power of leaders, are more likely to make hit-and-run guerrilla raids, using gossip and scorn as weapons, than they are to engage in public confrontations. It may be true that the best defense is a good offense, but leaders don't pick the time and circumstances of attacks upon them. At the outset of hostilities, these leaders are usually less prepared and less focused than their critics. The Blues often carry a sense of ambush—bitterness, personal hatred, tactics of slash and burn, and in the parlance of the current era, "the politics of personal destruction."

A large part of the nastiness that afflicts presidents appears to be the result of symbolic politics, of posturing and attack for the sheer pleasure of being seen on the campus as assertive or as capable of causing grief for persons in positions of leadership. These are not struggles over organizational survival or institutional integrity but local performances arising from anxiety over personal status or the desire to exercise bragging rights. We use these terms not in condemnation of any of the actors in the stories we have heard because, after all, we have heard only one perspective drawn from many-layered dramas. Yet, we can be reasonably sure that when the emotional stakes are high on one side of a controversy, they are likely to be comparably high on all sides.

Third, the levels of trust among participants are low. Paranoia is common and commonly justified. Each president with the Blues has a profound sense of being observed, of the smallest action and least consequential statement being reported and then repeated, often in ways that distort the intended meaning and ignores the context. Loyalty is in doubt. Fears and realizations of betrayal lurk at the edges of the Blues. Presidents have a sense that other people stand behind them but, upon reflection, they are not sure whether those who stand to their rear are there as friendly forces ready to enter the fray, or as potential allies for the enemy, or because there is less heat and controversy towards the rear. Leaders talk about loneliness and a sense of vulnerability: "Where are these attacks coming from and what is prompting them? Why me?" They recount the need for friendship, for family, for being connected to a personal life outside of the scene of conflict, incivility, and betrayal. They feel abandoned.

Fourth, the struggles feed upon themselves more than they feed upon any issues that they involve. There is the sense of being locked in a blood feud, where the original insult, perhaps unintended, is lost from the field of view and all that seems to matter in the next maneuver in a never-ending campaign to gain advantage. The lines of attack and the rhetoric of the opposition can often be traced to old enmities and skirmishes that were assumed to be long forgotten. Thus, memory plays a dual function: On the one hand, it is good for participants in the fight to know "where the bodies are buried," and who played on which team in recent battles. On the other hand, those who carry that knowledge are usually weighted down by lingering resentments and musty grudges that may obscure their view of how the field of contest may have changed in recent years and the fact that old loyalties may no longer be reliable.

A central feature of the Leadership Blues is a deep mismatch between the conceptions of individual leaders and key features of the organizations they lead. The leaders want to imagine that educational leadership is a noble calling through which people of intelligence and competence come together to guide a united college to shared educational objectives. They want to imagine that issues can be resolved by thoughtful discussion within a community of shared respect. Those imaginations are consistently contradicted by their experience. The organizations they lead are not only fractious with disagreements over what measures might lead to good educational outcomes, but profoundly torn with respect to their interpretations of educational objectives. They are characterized by very low levels of mutual trust. Academic institutions appear to be institutions of human beings with the usual human frailties—pettiness, selfishness, and sensitivity to imagined insult—frailties that often overcome, or at least obscure, desires to do good.

Over the long run, this mismatch between leader expectations and the reality of educational organizations may well be rectified. Leaders will adjust their conceptions, and education will recruit and retain the leaders it deserves. A long the way, administrators are likely to come to deal more effectively with the worlds in which they find themselves. They will stop having unrealistic expectations about their jobs, their associates, and themselves. Either through training or recruitment, colleges are likely to secure educational leaders who are effective operating under the unpleasant realities of administrative life, even finding leaders who enjoy the unpleasantness. Colleges will be led by leaders with few illusions about educational organizations and the people who inhabit them, who accept that there are few shared objectives and little basis for trust, and who thrive in such a world.

The politics of a campus is like the politics of a small town and presidents need to make deals. Even where a college campus is set in a large urban complex it still usually functions as a small town, living a life largely isolated from the media attention, political power and civic forces of the city that surrounds it. Thus, we observe the personal, and even petty, politics of a surprisingly small municipality even on a campus in the midst of a large city. Yet, by and large, college presidents are not trained as politicians, nor do they see themselves as such. Presidents look for allies among faculty, administrators, students or citizens in the surrounding community, and especially among members of their governing boards. But there seems little inclination to try log-rolling, the trading of support that can serve the highest priority of both presidents and their opponents.

The Blues also reveal a persistent dilemma associated with a leader's role in change. As a general rule, one does not enter the Administrator's Hall of Fame by presiding over the status quo no matter how pleasing the current stasis may be for many people associated with the campus, and no matter that a given change may well not be a good idea. The necessity of change is a mantra of leadership, as is the necessity of administrative leadership to effect change. As a result, administrators and other relatively short term participants in academic life have a persistent bias toward change.

A consistent theme in the Blues is the well-intended (but frustrated) initiation of change on the part of those in formal authority. For a new administrator, a driving force is the chance to make a mark on the organization and to build a record of innovative leadership that moves both the campus and the administrator toward their ambitions.

For more experienced members of the college community, the impulse to change on the part of administrators is likely to seem pretentious and self-interested. For them, and especially for the faculty and staff, the advent of a new administrator may simply be another dreary chapter in a long and frustrating story of management gimmicks (e.g. management by objectives or continuous quality improvement) and devotion to selfish ambition that, for too long, has provided justification for not listening to those who do vital work every day but who do not reside at the top of the administrative or governance hierarchy. Thus, we can expect on most campuses a severe disagreement about who are true patriots, the genuine adherents of the college's mission. Certainly we can observe on virtually every campus the chasms that separate the "faculty" from the "administration," on the one hand, and the "board" from the "administration," on the other.

These realities of leadership life invite some practical guidelines for college leaders who want to survive in the unpleasant world in which they find themselves. Our recommendation is that anyone who wants to be an administrator should leave his or her innocence behind. The job is not one that produces friends. Since much of the leadership of any institution is bound up in enforcing rules and saying "no," any administrator who wants a friend should buy a dog.

The primary administrative talent is not one of knowing how to make good decisions but of knowing how to manage impressions, making the institutions look good in the eyes of others and creating an illusion of direction and control. Those who sing the Blues tell us that it is important to maintain a pretense of confidence and strength, even when feeling uncertain and weak; that it is better to shift attention than to confront criticism; that the best strategy for an ambitious administrator is to depict oneself as the champion of uncontroversial changes to observers on campus (e.g. bigger budgets, higher salaries and nicer buildings) while appearing to eyes outside the campus as having engineered controversial changes in efficiency (e.g. reallocating resources, enforcing higher performance standards, cutting budgets to achieve efficiency, and eliminating "deadwood" from staff and faculty).

These guidelines of sophistication and manipulation make a certain amount of sense. By encouraging realistic expectations of leaders, they reduce the gap between expectations and experience. The gap can, however, be reduced in another way—at least in principle. We can change the reality, rather than the leaders' expectations about it.

In the short run, of course, organizational reality adapts relatively slowly, thus inviting changes in the selection and education of leaders. The Blues teach us about the powerful feedback mechanism between tactics and mistrust. A tactical reaction to lack of trust may permit survival, but it is a mean survival. It reinforces distrust and traps an organization and its leadership into continual warfare upon a terrain of fortresses. In effect, by seeking to train and select leaders who can adapt easily to unattractive worlds they encounter in their roles as leaders, we reduce the likelihood of inducing those worlds to adapt to the kinds of leaders that will ultimately serve us better.

The ability of the community colleges, an extraordinarily important branch of our educational system, to recruit constructive and humane professionals into the various roles of leadership is compromised by the nature of life portrayed here. It is a life from which decent people are likely to be repelled, rejecting the idea of serving as leaders of educational institutions rather than being attracted to the role. We can ask "How tough, thick-skinned and even ruthless must community college leaders be in order to survive in the petty world of campus politics?" If adherence to principles of decency and community is a disadvantage to community college leaders, then will only those without those principles be willing to serve? And if so, will this make the community college a less effective instrument of social and individual growth?

The point is not to try to eliminate conflict from colleges, for there are genuine issues on which reasonable people can thoughtfully disagree, but to reduce the destructive personalization and aggravation of conflict and to civilize the culture faced by campus leadership. What can be done?

- The issue of civility needs to be placed on the agenda of various groups on campus and state-wide associations. What is the reality of the issue? What harm is being done that is of concern to the campus as a whole? What forces are at work? What practical steps can be taken? In this respect, local boards of trustees and the state-wide trustee organizations can assume a particular leadership role because they hold ultimate responsibility for the health of the campus and they should be able to bring a degree of detachment to campus controversies. The state Chancellor can also bring attention to the issue as part of the challenge of building trust among state-level constituency groups and the accrediting commission can insist that "civility" is a necessary focus for self-study.
- Various avenues to build trust and resolve grievances—campus ombudsmen, special campus commissions on human relations, retreats involving trustees and campus leaders—need to be used more actively. Campuses are well advised to draw upon knowledge of conflict resolution techniques within their own faculties and the faculties of nearby institutions.

- Campus ceremonies and rituals can be used more widely as occasions for exhibiting mutual recognition and respect. Special days can be designated to recognize the roles of various groups on campus and to celebrate volunteer efforts. Campus assemblies can be organized that focus on the over-all mission of the college and bring back successful graduates to give praise and thanks.
- Campus publications can profile individuals and tell their stories of service. Better yet, administrators can write in praise of faculty and vice versa. Committee assignments and even job-sharing can be use as ways to build understanding of the challenges facing leaders on campus.

These are all small steps. They are probably of more use in preventing poisonous conflict than in resolving it. They are undoubtedly romantic in their hopes. In the final analysis, there is no quick fix, and there will be no end to conflict and pettiness. But just as gossip and scorn are effective techniques to demoralize and destroy, mutual respect and recognition are effective techniques to foster unity and the campus coherence necessary to carry on the important work of the community colleges.

Underlying these problems, moreover, are some grander ones. Why is the world of education filled with angry people engaging in gratuitous unpleasantness? Partly, the answer is that modern America is filled with angry people, and education cannot escape being part of that. We live in an incredibly successful and rich society in which many adults react to what seem to be minor insults with vitriol and violence.

But part of the answer lies within the education world and the community college itself. In a series of studies by himself and others, Roderick M. Kramer[4] has developed a set of ideas about

---

[4] Roderick M. Kramer, "Paranoid Cognition in Social Systems: Thinking and Acting in the Shadow of Doubt," *Personality and Social Psychology Review*, 2 (1998) 251-275.

the ways in which suspicions that others are exploiting, harming or deceiving one, doubts about the loyalty of trustworthiness of associates, and fears that information about oneself will be used against oneself lead to a cascade of distrust, sensitivity, and accusation that feed upon each other. In his formulation, paranoid-like reactions are generated not by individual pathologies but by social situations. His studies show how a tendency to attribute events to sinister others acting conspiratorially arises from a feeling that one is under intense evaluative scrutiny, which in turn arises from uncertainty about one's social status and a feeling of being different from others involved in the situation. One source of the feeling of being different is an emphasis on diversity rather than unity in a community, hyper consciousness of the ways in which people in a group differ. One source of uncertainty about one's social status is consciousness of being subordinate in power or authority relations.

In particular, it seems clear that it has become harder for people attached to colleges to see themselves as part of a serious community of similar individuals among whom concerns for the well-being of the institution are important and shared. They are more inclined to define their relations with the college as stemming from relatively narrow definitions of personal or group self-interest and to assume that others are similarly primarily concerned with themselves, thus not to be trusted. Teaching has become less a calling than a job. Administrators have become less reluctant servants of the institution than ambitious careerists. Boards have become less voices of altruistic hopes for learning than the manifestation s of particular interests and individual political ambitions.

A vision of a society based on the pursuit of individual and group distinctiveness in pursuit of self-interest is an honorable vision and one that captures an important part of the American spirit; but it has traditionally been combined, particularly in education, with a vision of obligations, community, and mutual civility.

There is an obvious tension between the two and maintaining each as a counterpoint to the other is far from easy. Contemporary American community college life is losing its sense of mission and community, and thereby its civility, to an excess of personal and subgroup differentiation and gratification that generate fears that everyone else is trying to put something over on us.

Most community college presidents were attracted to leadership out of a commitment to the educational and social ideals of the community colleges. Their hard work has brought them knowledge of their institutions as a whole. They have experienced the joy of observing the internal workings of a complex mechanism even if the gears and levers have resisted change and occasionally have injured them seriously. They have made difficult forays into campus politics, have suffered for them, but have survived. They have succeeded in helping individuals in a myriad of ways. The good news is that idealists persist and the occasional presidential ogre is detected and fired, either sooner or later.

Leadership Blues are a reminder that however much a social system may treasure those who persist in serving the common good in the face of major penalties for doing so, civilization requires civility and will not long survive if its governance attracts only those who are cunning and combative. Leaders will be held accountable for many things over which they have little or no control. That is understood. General Yamashita was executed by the American army on February 23, 1946. But if the daily activities of leadership are corrupted by pettiness and indecency, then only the indecent and petty will find them appealing.

www.ingramcontent.com/pod-product-compliance
Lightning Source LLC
Chambersburg PA
CBHW052052090426
42739CB00010B/2142